INCREASING STUDENT SUCCESS IN DEVELOPMENTAL MATHEMATICS

PROCEEDINGS OF A WORKSHOP

Linda Casola and Tiffany E. Taylor, *Rapporteurs*

Board on Science Education

Division of Behavioral and Social Sciences and Education

Board on Mathematical Sciences and Analytics

Division on Engineering and Physical Sciences

The National Academies of
SCIENCES · ENGINEERING · MEDICINE

THE NATIONAL ACADEMIES PRESS
Washington, DC
www.nap.edu

THE NATIONAL ACADEMIES PRESS 500 Fifth Street, NW Washington, DC 20001

This activity was supported by a contract awarded to the National Academy of Sciences and Ascendium Education Group (unnumbered). Any opinions, findings, conclusions, or recommendations expressed in this publication do not necessarily reflect the views of any organization or agency that provided support for the project.

International Standard Book Number-13: 978-0-309-49662-9
International Standard Book Number-10: 0-309-49662-4
Digital Object Identifier: https://doi.org/10.17226/25547

Additional copies of this publication are available from the National Academies Press, 500 Fifth Street, NW, Keck 360, Washington, DC 20001; (800) 624-6242 or (202) 334-3313; http://www.nap.edu.

Copyright 2019 by the National Academy of Sciences. All rights reserved.

Printed in the United States of America

Suggested citation: National Academies of Sciences, Engineering, and Medicine. (2019). *Increasing Student Success in Developmental Mathematics: Proceedings of a Workshop*. Washington, DC: The National Academies Press. https://doi.org/10.17226/25547.

The National Academies of
SCIENCES · ENGINEERING · MEDICINE

The **National Academy of Sciences** was established in 1863 by an Act of Congress, signed by President Lincoln, as a private, nongovernmental institution to advise the nation on issues related to science and technology. Members are elected by their peers for outstanding contributions to research. Dr. Marcia McNutt is president.

The **National Academy of Engineering** was established in 1964 under the charter of the National Academy of Sciences to bring the practices of engineering to advising the nation. Members are elected by their peers for extraordinary contributions to engineering. Dr. John L. Anderson is president.

The **National Academy of Medicine** (formerly the Institute of Medicine) was established in 1970 under the charter of the National Academy of Sciences to advise the nation on medical and health issues. Members are elected by their peers for distinguished contributions to medicine and health. Dr. Victor J. Dzau is president.

The three Academies work together as the **National Academies of Sciences, Engineering, and Medicine** to provide independent, objective analysis and advice to the nation and conduct other activities to solve complex problems and inform public policy decisions. The National Academies also encourage education and research, recognize outstanding contributions to knowledge, and increase public understanding in matters of science, engineering, and medicine.

Learn more about the National Academies of Sciences, Engineering, and Medicine at **www.nationalacademies.org**.

The National Academies of
SCIENCES • ENGINEERING • MEDICINE

Consensus Study Reports published by the National Academies of Sciences, Engineering, and Medicine document the evidence-based consensus on the study's statement of task by an authoring committee of experts. Reports typically include findings, conclusions, and recommendations based on information gathered by the committee and the committee's deliberations. Each report has been subjected to a rigorous and independent peer-review process and it represents the position of the National Academies on the statement of task.

Proceedings published by the National Academies of Sciences, Engineering, and Medicine chronicle the presentations and discussions at a workshop, symposium, or other event convened by the National Academies. The statements and opinions contained in proceedings are those of the participants and are not endorsed by other participants, the planning committee, or the National Academies.

For information about other products and activities of the National Academies, please visit www.nationalacademies.org/about/whatwedo.

PLANNING COMMITTEE FOR THE WORKSHOP ON INCREASING STUDENT SUCCESS IN DEVELOPMENTAL MATHEMATICS

HOWARD GOBSTEIN (*Chair*), Association of Public & Land-grant Universities
SUSAN BICKERSTAFF, Community College Research Center, Columbia University
LINDA BRADDY, Tarrant County College
TRISTAN DENLEY, University System of Georgia
JAMES DORSEY, College Success Foundation
TATIANA MELGUIZO, University of Southern California
VILMA MESA, University of Michigan
JULIE PHELPS, Valencia College, East Campus
PHILIP URI TREISMAN, Charles A. Dana Center, The University of Texas at Austin

TIFFANY E. TAYLOR, *Study Director*
KERRY BRENNER, *Senior Program Officer*
HEIDI SCHWEINGRUBER, *Director, Board on Science Education*
MICHELLE SCHWALBE, *Director, Board on Mathematical Sciences and Analytics*
JESSICA COVINGTON, *Senior Program Assistant*

BOARD ON SCIENCE EDUCATION

ADAM GAMORAN (*Chair*), William T. Grant Foundation, New York
MEGAN BANG, School of Education and Social Policy, Northwestern University
VICKI L. CHANDLER, Minerva Schools at Keck Graduate Institute
SUNITA V. COOKE, MiraCosta College, Oceanside, CA
RUSH D. HOLT, American Association for the Advancement of Science, Washington, DC
MATTHEW KREHBIEL, Achieve, Inc.
CATHRYN (CATHY) MANDUCA, Science Education Resource Center, Carleton College
JOHN MATHER, NASA Goddard Space Flight Center
TONYA M. MATTHEWS, Wayne State University
WILLIAM PENUEL, School of Education, University of Colorado Boulder
STEPHEN L. PRUITT, Southern Regional Education Board
K. RENAE PULLEN, Caddo Parish Schools, Shreveport, LA
K. ANN RENNINGER, Department of Educational Studies, Swarthmore College
MARSHALL "MIKE" SMITH, Carnegie Foundation for the Advancement of Teaching
MARCY H. TOWNS, Department of Chemistry, Purdue University

HEIDI SCHWEINGRUBER, *Director*

BOARD ON MATHEMATICAL SCIENCES AND ANALYTICS

STEPHEN M. ROBINSON (*Chair*), University of Wisconsin–Madison
JOHN R. BIRGE, University of Chicago
W. PETER CHERRY, Independent Consultant
DAVID S.C. CHU, Institute for Defense Analyses
RONALD R. COIFMAN, Yale University
JAMES (JIM) CURRY, University of Colorado Boulder
MARK L. GREEN, University of California, Los Angeles
SHAWNDRA HILL, Microsoft Research
LYDIA KAVRAKI, Rice University
TAMARA KOLDA, Sandia National Laboratories
JOSEPH A. LANGSAM, University of Maryland, College Park
DAVID MAIER, Portland State University
LOIS CURFMAN McINNES, Argonne National Laboratory
JILL PIPHER, Brown University
ELIZABETH A. THOMPSON, University of Washington
CLAIRE TOMLIN, University of California, Berkeley
LANCE WALLER, Emory University
KAREN E. WILLCOX, The University of Texas at Austin
DAVID YAO, Columbia University

MICHELLE SCHWALBE, *Director*

Acknowledgment of Reviewers

This Proceedings of a Workshop was reviewed in draft form by individuals chosen for their diverse perspectives and technical expertise. The purpose of this independent review is to provide candid and critical comments that will assist the National Academies of Sciences, Engineering, and Medicine in making each published proceedings as sound as possible and to ensure that it meets the institutional standards for quality, objectivity, evidence, and responsiveness to the charge. The review comments and draft manuscript remain confidential to protect the integrity of the process.

We thank the following individuals for their review of this workshop proceedings: Helen E. Burn, Department of Mathematics and Curriculum Research Group, Highline College; Ted Coe, Mathematics, Achieve, Inc.; Tristan Denley, Academic Affairs, University System of Georgia; and Thai-Huy Nguyen, College of Education, Seattle University.

Although the reviewers listed above provided many constructive comments and suggestions, they were not asked to endorse the content of the proceedings nor did they see the final draft before its release. The review of this proceedings was overseen by George R. Boggs, Superintendent/President Emeritus, Palomar College. He was responsible for making certain that an independent examination of this proceedings was carried out in accordance with standards of the National Academies and that all review comments were carefully considered. Responsibility for the final content rests entirely with the rapporteurs and the National Academies.

Contents

1	Introduction	1
2	The Current Landscape of Developmental Mathematics Education	11
3	Developmental Mathematics Students and Their Experiences	31
4	Promising Approaches for Transforming Developmental Mathematics Education	55
5	Building Capacity to Meet the Needs of Students	73
6	Vision for the Future and Possible Next Steps	83
7	References	89

Appendixes

A	Workshop Agenda	93
B	Biographical Sketches of Workshop Planning Committee Members and Presenters	99
C	Workshop Participants	109

1

Introduction

The Board on Science Education and the Board on Mathematical Sciences and Analytics of the National Academies of Sciences, Engineering, and Medicine convened the Workshop on Increasing Student Success in Developmental Mathematics, March 18–19, 2019, at the National Academy of Sciences building in Washington, DC. This workshop explored how to best support *all* students in postsecondary mathematics, with particular attention to students who are unsuccessful in developmental mathematics and with an eye toward issues of access to promising reforms and equitable learning environments.

GOALS OF THE WORKSHOP

The 2-day workshop was designed to bring together a variety of stakeholders, including experts who have developed and/or implemented new initiatives to improve the mathematics education experience for students. The overarching goal of the workshop was to take stock of the mathematics education community's progress in this domain, as guided by the questions in the planning committee's Statement of Task (see Box 1-1). Participants (i.e., workshop planning committee members, presenters, and attendees) examined the data on students who are well served by new reform structures in developmental mathematics and discussed various cohorts of students who are not currently well served—(1) those who even with access to reforms do not succeed and (2) those who do not have access to a reform due to differential access constraints. Throughout the workshop, participants also explored promising approaches to bolstering student outcomes

> **BOX 1-1**
> **Statement of Task**
>
> A planning committee will plan a 2-day open workshop that will explore the effectiveness of postsecondary developmental (remedial) mathematics courses, with particular attention to the students who are unsuccessful in these courses. The workshop will explore the challenges these students face, promising approaches, and areas where additional research is needed.
>
> The workshop will focus on the following questions:
>
> 1. Which students are well served by the current offerings in developmental mathematics? How do we define "well served" and what are indicators of student success in developmental mathematics? How do we define which students are included here?
> 2. What is the size of the total population that is not well served? Are there subgroups within this group and how do needs or challenges vary across them? How do Adult Basic Education students fit in?
> 3. What is known about why some students are not well served? What do we need to know in order to serve them better?
> 4. Are there examples of successful approaches? What are the components of these programs (considering interventions both within and outside of the classroom)? What is needed in order to implement the more successful approaches?
> 5. What are the potential challenges and what strategies can be used to address them? What are the next steps?
> 6. What are the gaps in the research base and what are the key directions for research, both short and long term?
>
> After the workshop, a Proceedings of a Workshop of the presentations and discussions at the workshop will be prepared by a designated rapporteur in accordance with institutional guidelines.

in mathematics, focusing especially on research and data that demonstrate the success of these approaches; deliberated and discussed barriers and opportunities for effectively serving all students; and outlined some key directions of inquiry intended to address the prevailing research and data needs in the field.

ORGANIZATION OF THIS PROCEEDINGS

This workshop was organized by an independent planning committee in accordance with the procedures of the National Academies. The planning committee's role was limited to setting the agenda and convening the workshop. (See Appendix A for the workshop agenda, Appendix B for biographical information for the planning committee members and workshop presenters, and Appendix C for the full list of in-person workshop participants.) This proceedings summarizes the discussions that occurred throughout the workshop and highlights key points raised during the presentations, moderated panel discussions, and small group discussions among the workshop participants. This chapter outlines the scope of the workshop, including the goals, guiding questions, and an opening discussion on the importance of mathematics education. Chapter 2 presents the current landscape of developmental mathematics education, with attention to reform efforts and equity concerns. Chapter 3 describes student demographics and course-taking experiences in developmental mathematics, with specific data and commentary on what works for whom across four diverse state contexts. Chapter 4 discusses promising models for change in developmental mathematics education, with consideration for the context of broader transformations in undergraduate education. Chapter 5 presents strategies to build capacity for continuous educational improvement. Chapter 6 highlights participants' ideas for next steps and a vision for the future of developmental mathematics education.[1]

In accordance with the policies of the National Academies, this proceedings was prepared by the workshop rapporteurs as a factual summary of what occurred at the workshop. The workshop did not attempt to establish any conclusions or recommendations about needs and future directions, focusing instead on issues identified by the workshop presenters and participants. Statements, recommendations, and opinions expressed are those of individual presenters and participants, do not represent the views of all workshop participants or the planning committee, and are not necessarily endorsed or verified by the National Academies. They should not be construed as reflecting any group consensus.

WELCOMING REMARKS

Howard Gobstein, workshop planning committee chair and executive vice president of research, innovation, and science, technology, engineering, and mathematics (STEM) policy at the Association of Public & Land-grant Universities, described developmental mathematics education as "one of the most pressing education issues" of this era and emphasized that mathematics continues to be a barrier to degree completion for many students, particularly for students of color. Barriers to learning mathematics, he

---

[1] Videos of presentations and additional materials prepared or compiled for this workshop can be found at http://sites.nationalacademies.org/DBASSE/BOSE/Developmental_Math/index.htm.

continued, can severely limit opportunities for hundreds of thousands of students, as success in mathematics relates to postsecondary enrollment, career advancement, financial stability and upward mobility, quality of life, and societal contributions.

Gobstein explained that recent research on and reforms to developmental mathematics education, as well as the engagement of dedicated faculty, policy makers, and administrators, has increased the number of students able to succeed in their first credit-bearing mathematics course. However, despite this progress, he continued, a significant portion of students are still not succeeding in mathematics. Gobstein asserted that the system is failing these students, and "the problem is magnified as many of these students are becoming the majority population in the United States as their demographics shift." This issue, then, is also "about the equitable future of our country … [and] understanding mathematics is foundational to helping to address this." The mathematics education community, he continued, is faced with a substantial challenge; but with a better understanding of how to best serve students via the promising reforms under way, it is possible to eliminate existing barriers and reach the remaining cohorts of students.

In addition to the goals of the workshop already discussed above, Gobstein raised more specific guiding questions to be considered over the course of the 2-day workshop:

- What do we know about present student success? What works well, where, and for whom?
- For whom does it not work? What do we know about the students who are not currently well served, and where are they?
- What do we need to do to significantly broaden student success? What more do we need to know both to advance progress and to keep track of our improvements?
- What is involved to move the field from individual programmatic attempts to systemic changes at scale and to make this normative to the system (i.e., how to eliminate the mathematics barrier for students and make "no barrier" the new normal)?

He reiterated that it is important to the mathematics education community, and to the nation as a whole, to eliminate the mathematics barrier that often constrains the education and career decisions of hundreds of thousands, perhaps millions, of students each year. Gobstein concluded his remarks by saying that this workshop is an opportunity to convey to many stakeholders, and to the nation more broadly, the important next steps in this field.

THE VALUE OF MATHEMATICS EDUCATION AND THE NEED FOR REFORM

Linda Braddy, former deputy executive director of the Mathematical Association of America (MAA) and current vice president for academic affairs at Tarrant County College (a community college in Texas), moderated the workshop's opening panel discussion. Joined by two mathematics professors, she invited conversation on the importance of mathematics education, the role that mathematics plays in the student experience, and the need for developmental mathematics reforms to increase success for all students. During her tenure at MAA, Braddy co-wrote *A Common Vision for Undergraduate Mathematical Sciences Programs in 2025*[2] and the *MAA Instructional Practices Guide*,[3] two national documents reflecting efforts by the mathematics societies, in particular, to create vehicles for assessing where consensus exists around teaching and learning mathematics.

Trained as a pure mathematician, panelist Mark Green is professor emeritus of mathematics at the University of California, Los Angeles (UCLA). Owing to his experience leading the National Science Foundation (NSF)-sponsored Institute for Pure and Applied Mathematics that fosters interactions in mathematics and other disciplines, his expertise lies in the intellectual footprint of mathematics, broadly speaking. He is also the incoming chair of the Board on Mathematical Sciences and Analytics at the National Academies.

With 41 years of teaching experience, panelist Paula Wilhite was a charter faculty member and is now division chair of mathematics, physics, and engineering at Northeast Texas Community College, an institution that serves a significant percentage of Hispanic students.[4] She also serves as the chair of the Developmental Mathematics Committee of the American Mathematical Association of Two-Year Colleges (AMATYC), a committee of nearly 400 members.

Reflecting on current perceptions of mathematics education, Braddy, Green, and Wilhite agreed that traditional approaches to developmental mathematics education (i.e., algebra-calculus pathway), in particular, have proven to be ineffective for an increasing number of students (see Chen, 2016). Additionally, Braddy shared what she referred to as a "striking statistic": only 10 to 15 percent of jobs require the intense use of college algebra or Algebra 2 from high school. Struck by how low that percentage

---

[2]For more information about *A Common Vision for Undergraduate Mathematical Sciences Programs in 2025*, see https://www.maa.org/sites/default/files/pdf/CommonVisionFinal.pdf.

[3]For more information about the *MAA Instructional Practices Guide*, see https://www.maa.org/sites/default/files/InstructPracGuide_web.pdf.

[4]For more information about enrollment at Northeast Texas Community College by race/ethnicity, see https://datausa.io/profile/university/northeast-texas-community-college#enrollment.

is, she asserted that more innovative mathematics pathways that provide alternatives to the algebra pathway are needed to reach the masses of students who need strong mathematics competencies and analytical skills in preparation for careers that do not necessarily require a STEM degree.

Green pointed out that although UCLA has a general quantitative requirement for all students, a growing number of majors specifically require mathematics and/or statistics credits. For example, life sciences requires calculus and statistics; physical sciences, engineering, and climate sciences require mathematics; psychology, sociology, political science, public affairs, international development studies, global studies, and communication require statistics; and cognitive science, neuroscience, psychobiology, economics, business economics, and the science-focused anthropology track all require both mathematics and statistics credits. Furthermore, he continued, as workforce needs evolve alongside the emergence of new disciplines, the mathematical skill sets that students need will continue to change. He added that the stakes are high for students and their future opportunities will be limited if they do not know mathematics.

Braddy explained that the principle behind multiple mathematics pathways, a common developmental mathematics reform approach, is that students will be more prepared for future opportunities by taking the specific types of mathematics tailored to their respective careers. She endorsed the notion of evolving multiple mathematics pathways beyond the current algebra/calculus, statistics, or quantitative reasoning pathways to appreciate different focuses of the mathematics, such as for nursing and the health sciences where communicating effectively with mathematical language is an important skill set. Wilhite shared that Northeast Texas Community College has implemented multiple mathematics pathways for students as a way to provide the variety of mathematics that is needed to fulfill the requirements of each major. Each mathematics pathway "opens up the world to a different set of students," Green shared. Students with strong inductive reasoning skills might be attracted to statistics courses; students with strong critical thinking skills and a curiosity for real-world problems might take an interest in mathematical modeling; and students drawn to programming would benefit from courses that stress algorithmic thinking. He referenced the National Research Council (2013) report *The Mathematical Sciences in 2025*, noting that how well a student learns mathematical concepts is also directly influenced by how interested he/she is in those concepts and how they relate to who the student hopes to become in the future. Without access to the appropriate postsecondary-level mathematics pathways and related skill sets, students could be limited in terms of their career options and opportunities for upward mobility, Green reiterated.

Wilhite emphasized that implementation of mathematics reforms, such as multiple mathematics pathways, is not without its challenges and criticisms. Many "naysayers," she explained, believe that multiple mathematics pathways limit students' opportunities for advanced courses or careers in STEM and that they do not offer the same level of rigor as college algebra. However, she stressed that forcing all first-year students to take college algebra is what truly limits students' opportunities for the future. Braddy added that data can be used to demonstrate to the "naysayers" that reforms help students by eliminating barriers that affect career goals and potential for upward mobility.

In preparing to implement mathematics education reforms, Wilhite shared that institutional leaders should consider how to do the following: evaluate students' progress, understand what it means to succeed in each type of mathematics, support students who change majors, and adapt faculty training and staffing levels. She highlighted several staffing challenges related to the implementation of the co-requisite reform model, in particular, but underscored that "none of these challenges is insurmountable." The co-requisite model is a shift from the longer developmental mathematics sequence; students are placed directly into college-level courses that are paired with support(s) (e.g., tutoring, combining a developmental course with a college-level course, and/or stretching one course over two semesters to allow students to complete the course at a slower pace). Wilhite explained that this often presents a scheduling challenge, in that the model tends to prompt particularly large enrollments in the fall semester and smaller enrollments in the spring semester. Institutions, she continued, could provide balance by addressing English co-requisites in the fall and mathematics in the spring as one approach to overcoming staffing issues.

Another challenge for staffing noted by Wilhite relates to the expertise and qualifications of mathematics instructors. Given the nature of the nation's data-driven economy, Wilhite wholeheartedly supports including statistical analysis in mathematics curricula; however, she expressed concern about how to staff these courses, since many instructors are not adequately prepared to teach statistical analysis. The American Mathematical Society and the MAA released a statement in 2014 that begins to address this gap: It recommends that instructors should have extensive experience with statistical analysis and a minimum of two courses on their transcripts that prepare them to teach statistical methods in an introductory statistics course. Green described a similar concern about recruiting qualified faculty to teach new courses in big data, which are emerging as part of undergraduate curricula across the United States (e.g., the University of California, Berkeley's Data8, an exploratory course in big data). Experts in big data tend to avoid teaching careers, given the more attractive opportunities that exist in industry. However, joint appointments, in which experts would spend half of their time teaching and half of their time working in industry, could address this potential faculty shortage, Green explained. Braddy agreed that institutional leaders should anticipate and consider how to address the challenges that will arise from scaling mathematics pathways programs, which requires the addition of more courses and more qualified instructors. She added that although relying on adjunct faculty is not the optimal solution for staffing problems for a variety of reasons—they often receive low pay and have poor working conditions—adjunct faculty are often mathematics practitioners who have unique expertise that is incredibly beneficial for students. Furthermore, she continued, mathematics departments could also draw on resources and training from the NSF-supported MAA initiative StatPrep,[5] which has created hubs in and around urban community colleges to help mathematics faculty become more proficient in teaching modern statistics.

Panelists invited audience members to share their questions and observations about the importance of mathematics education and mathematics education reform. Vilma Mesa, professor of education and mathematics at the University of Michigan, observed the limited number of changes that have occurred in mathematics education during the past 50 years. She emphasized that problems within the field of mathematics education are very difficult to solve. Green echoed Mesa's concerns and noted that the pace of change in higher education is "glacial," at best, referencing the 15 years that it took from the awareness of the need for a course in big data at UCLA in 2004 to finally receiving approval to implement a data theory track in 2019. In order to better understand how to revise mathematics curricula, more conversations are needed about the institutional constraints that determine which students take which courses, Mesa asserted. Philip Uri Treisman, founder and executive director of the Charles A. Dana Center at The University of Texas at Austin,[6] emphasized the need to monitor the growing need for quantitative competency through the mathematical sciences in undergraduate and graduate education, and Green proposed that the mathematics community should conduct decadal studies to better document the educational implications of mathematics, including specific uses of mathematics in other fields.

Before the panel concluded its discussion, Wilhite introduced the topic of academic rigor in mathematics courses, endorsing The University of Texas at Austin Charles A. Dana Center's statement that "rigor in mathematics is a set of skills that centers on the communication and the use of mathematical language" (Charles A. Dana Center, 2019). Green championed this definition of rigor and pointed out that each type of mathematics

---

[5]For more information about StatPrep, see http://statprep.org.

[6]The mission of the Dana Center is to "support seamless transitions for all students" by "creating pathways for success" and providing "support at every level." For more information, see https://www.utdanacenter.org/who-we-are/our-mission.

has a standard of what it means to understand concepts and perform tasks well. Supporting Wilhite's earlier declaration that pathways actually *expand* choices for students, Treisman wondered whether evidence from students' transcripts exists to identify the career options available to students who have completed college algebra, which would support the notion that college algebra actually keeps students' options open to be engineers or mathematicians. Treisman noted that his own research shows almost no students graduating with a degree in engineering or mathematics who took college algebra or precalculus as a college student; significantly more students take calculus in high school and are therefore entering college with richer mathematics backgrounds than was the case 10 or 15 years ago. Wilhite agreed that students who complete college algebra rarely move on to take another college-level mathematics course such as calculus. In fact, college algebra is considered a terminal course, with very few exceptions, she continued. Braddy reiterated that because many students are not served well by the current approach to mathematics education (i.e., the college algebra pathway), which can impact career decisions, the need for reform becomes even more important.

2

The Current Landscape of Developmental Mathematics Education

Rapid change is occurring in the developmental mathematics education reform space as institutional leaders, faculty members, researchers, and policy makers work to create learning environments that enable more students to be successful in mathematics (U.S. Department of Education, 2017). During the second and third sessions of the workshop, participants exchanged insights on the current research on and implementation of developmental mathematics education reforms that could help institutions determine what data, support, and infrastructure they need to best meet the needs of their students, especially those from underrepresented populations. Additionally, the current strategies for creating equitable opportunities for all students were discussed.

STRATEGIES TO IMPROVE DEVELOPMENTAL MATHEMATICS EDUCATION

Elizabeth Zachry Rutschow, a senior research associate at MDRC, who has led numerous research projects on developmental education, provided an overview of "Developmental Mathematics Reforms," a paper commissioned by the workshop planning committee on the range of developmental mathematics reforms being implemented and evaluated at 2- and 4-year institutions across the United States. She highlighted the most common reform models and discussed the students they target, their relative scale, and current research documenting their positive or negative effects on student outcomes.

> "Approximately 59 percent of students from 2-year institutions and 33 percent of students from 4-year institutions take developmental mathematics courses."

Zachry Rutschow opened her presentation by describing developmental education as coursework that students complete to build their skills prior to enrolling in college-level courses. Typically, these semester-long and often multicourse sequences are offered in mathematics, English, and reading; they are generally non-credit bearing and nontransferable (i.e., they do not count toward a college degree); and they are a costly undertaking for students, who, on average, take two to three successive courses. Approximately 59 percent of students from 2-year institutions and 33 percent of students from 4-year institutions take developmental mathematics courses. Yet, no common standards exist across institutions for how these courses should be taught, structured, or sequenced, and there are varying philosophies as to how students should be evaluated for appropriate course placement. In addition to the above information, Zachry Rutschow shared recent research that revealed that less than 58 percent of students who start developmental mathematics sequences finish them, and only 20 percent of those students successfully complete a college-level mathematics course. Low-income students and students from underrepresented groups are overrepresented in developmental education, and a significant number of students have been incorrectly placed in developmental courses (i.e., students who might have been successful in college-level courses are actually being placed in developmental education courses). To this end, she continued, policy makers, practitioners, and researchers have been motivated to consider new approaches to developmental education in order to improve student success.

Of the new approaches, Zachry Rutschow described five sets of reforms that are currently being offered to students in developmental mathematics education: assessment and placement, structure and sequence, instruction and content, student support, and comprehensive (see Box 2-1). Some overlap exists among these reform categories, some reforms are implemented together, and similar reforms are being implemented in English and reading curricula to serve students in need of multiple developmental education courses. To examine the impact of these reforms on student outcomes, Zachry Rutschow synthesized data from descriptive, quasi-experimental (QE), and randomized control trial (RCT) studies.

> **BOX 2-1**
> **Developmental Mathematics Education Reform At-A-Glance**
>
> Assessment and Placement Reforms
> - Diagnostic assessment
> - Early assessment
> - Multiple measures assessment
>
> Structure and Sequence Reforms
> - Intensive non-course-based alternatives
> - Compression models
> - Co-requisite models
>
> Instruction and Content Reforms
> - High-quality instruction
> - Cohort models and learning communities
> - Self-paced instruction
> - Multiple mathematics pathways
>
> Student Support Reforms
> - Success courses
> - Supplemental instruction
> - Tutoring
>
> Comprehensive Reforms
> - Guided pathways
> - Wrap-around support models
>
> SOURCE: Adapted from Zachry Rutschow (2019).

Assessment and Placement Reforms

Given that students are often incorrectly placed into developmental courses and often fail to progress to credit-bearing courses, Zachry Rutschow shared that various types of assessment and placement reforms are being implemented to mitigate these outcomes. One reform approach to the assessment and placement process is the use of diagnostic assessments (e.g., the ALEKS or ASSET exams) to identify student-specific strengths and weaknesses and to place students appropriately in modular or self-paced courses to strengthen particular skills. According to the research reviewed by Zachry Rutschow, the target group for diagnostic assessments varies. While all students could benefit from this approach, she explained that it may prove particularly useful for students with high scores on general placement exams and students in need of support across multiple disciplines. QE studies indicated that diagnostic assessments placed students more accurately than computer adaptive tests, but little research exists on the impacts of diagnostic assessments on students' overall academic progress. Because diagnostic assessments are often grouped with other assessments used to evaluate students' levels of college readiness, Zachry Rutschow explained that it can be difficult to discern the exact scale at which diagnostic assessments are being implemented. Despite this, she continued, it is known that academic institutions in Florida, Kentucky, North Carolina, North Dakota, Texas, and Virginia currently use diagnostic assessments.

Another type of assessment and placement reform is early assessment, which is targeted to high school students who may not be ready for college—for example, students who score below a 19 on the ACT. These students then have the opportunity to develop needed skills during their junior and senior years of high school, typically through an online tutorial course or in a more traditional classroom. As of 2017, this reform was being implemented at the programmatic level in high schools in 39 states (e.g., the Tennessee Seamless Alignment and Integrated Learning Support [SAILS] Program[1] and the California Early Assessment Program[2]), according to Zachry Rutschow. Descriptive studies in Arkansas and Mississippi found that early assessment increased students' skills and the likelihood of *placement* into college-level mathematics courses, but QE studies in California, Florida, and Tennessee suggested that this intervention might not lead to *completion* of higher college-level mathematics courses, Zachry Rutschow explained.

As evidenced in Zachry Rutschow's examination of the research, traditional standardized tests have not been shown to be good indicators of college readiness or success. Multiple measures assessment is a third type of assessment and placement reform that evaluates college readiness by bringing in additional measures of students' skills to consider alongside standardized test results. Often these include a student's high school performance—for example, grade point average, highest level of a course taken, number of courses taken per subject area, and, in some cases, noncognitive indicators, such as a student's motivation, academic commitment, and/or awareness of his/her own skills. Zachry Rutschow's synthesis illustrated that multiple measures assessments could be valuable for all students entering postsecondary institutions but could be particularly useful for recent high school graduates, students who earn high scores on standardized

---

[1] For more information about the Tennessee SAILS Program, see https://www.tn.gov/thec/bureaus/academic-affairs-and-student-success/academic-programs/sails.html and Chapter 3 of this proceedings.
[2] For more information about the California Early Assessment Program, see https://www.cde.ca.gov/ci/gs/hs/eapindex.asp.

tests, and adult learners. A total of 19 states permit and promote the use of multiple measures assessments for incoming students.[3] A national survey in 2016[4] indicated that multiple measures assessments were used in 57 percent of public 2-year institutions across the United States. Zachry Rutschow shared early results from an RCT study conducted at the State University of New York by the Center for the Analysis of Postsecondary Readiness, which showed that students are more likely to be placed into and complete a college-level mathematics course as a result of the multiple measures assessment reform. Additionally, she shared that a QE study in Florida—a state in which using students' high school grades to evaluate college readiness is mandatory—showed that students with higher levels of high school preparation succeeded more often in college-level courses, which, she stated, could make a compelling case for offering the multiple measures assessment.

Structure and Sequence Reforms

Zachry Rutschow asserted that students often have to take too many developmental courses for too long, which creates too many opportunities for students to drop out before completion. Instead, she continued, boot camps and other non-course-based options (e.g., summer bridge programs) could be useful to build students' skills through brief, intensive instruction offered outside of the traditional semester sequence, with the goal of placing students directly into a college-level mathematics course upon completion. Boot camps and non-course-based options are primarily targeted toward students who have already been evaluated as needing developmental education. These reforms are being fully implemented in Colorado, Connecticut, Kentucky, Mississippi, and Texas, though many individual institutions in other states are also offering similar alternatives for students. Zachry Rutschow shared the results of a 2012 RCT study of summer bridge programs in eight Texas community colleges, which indicated positive short-term effects on students' enrollment in and completion of college-level courses but fewer positive effects on long-term success throughout college. Additionally, she noted that a 2010 QE study of a 5-week summer bridge program at a 4-year institution suggested more promising long-term positive effects on students' graduation rates.

The compression of developmental course material into shorter time periods (e.g., offering two developmental education courses to be completed

---
[3]See Chapter 3 of this proceedings to learn more about a case study on the successful use of multiple measures assessments in California.
[4]Center for the Analysis of Postsecondary Readiness Institutional Survey (2016); for more information on this survey, see Zachry Rutschow and Mayer (2018).

in one semester, instead of two) is another type of structure and sequence reform highlighted by Zachry Rutschow. She noted that the target student group for this reform varies, but that 51 percent of public 2-year institutions were offering this option as of 2016 (e.g., Community College of Denver's FastStart Program[5]), and three states embedded this option as part of their policies and practices for community colleges. Descriptive studies demonstrated that compressed courses lead to an increase in successful completion of developmental education courses, and a QE study on the Community College of Denver's FastStart Program demonstrated an increase in the likelihood of students completing a college-level mathematics course within 3 years as compared to their peers, who were not placed in compressed courses.

The co-requisite model, Zachry Rutschow explained, is another innovative approach to reforming course structure. In this case, students are placed directly into college-level courses that are paired with support(s) (e.g., tutoring, combining a developmental course with a college-level course, and/or stretching one course over two semesters to allow students to complete the course at a slower pace). Although this reform was originally targeted to students with mathematics skills just below the respective placement test cutoff score, it is expanding to include students at all levels of developmental mathematics, Zachry Rutschow explained. This increasingly popular reform is either mandated or recommended for 2-year institutions in at least 15 states. An RCT study at the City University of New York (CUNY) indicated higher pass rates in college-level mathematics courses and higher rates of accumulation of college credits as a result of students' enrollment in the co-requisite model. Zachry Rutschow asserted that the co-requisite model seems to be the most encouraging reform of course structure and sequence undertaken to move students more quickly and successfully through developmental coursework and college-level coursework (see Chapter 4 for a deeper look at the co-requisite model).

Instruction and Content Reforms

Zachry Rutschow commented that mathematics course content is often misaligned with students' college and career goals, and traditional modes of instruction in mathematics have not led to conceptual understanding for students. A broad reform to address this problem, she explained, has been the use of high-quality instructional practices that are intended to build all students' conceptual knowledge through active learning, contextualized problem solving, and student-led solution methods. This approach,

---

[5]For more information about the Community College of Denver's FastStart Program, see https://files.eric.ed.gov/fulltext/ED521421.pdf.

she continued, is recommended by a number of national mathematics and higher education organizations, owing in part to promising research results. For example, a descriptive study demonstrated that students were more likely to earn higher scores in mathematics and to describe the instruction as "useful" when faculty employed contextualized instructional models, which focus on deep conceptual learning that is contextualized within real-life situations and afford better understanding of how mathematics can be applied in practical life. Zachry Rutschow's review of the research revealed a recent QE study of the Integrated Basic Education and Skills Training (IBEST) Program in Washington and other similar programs, which showed that both college credit and professional certificate accumulations increased for students who had received high-quality instruction; a recent RCT study of programs similar to IBEST revealed positive effects on both students' academic outcomes and their labor market outcomes.

The implementation of cohort-based design instruction (i.e., learning communities) was an early instructional reform effort that typically paired two courses (e.g., two developmental-level courses or one developmental mathematics course with a college-level course). In more intensive versions of the approach, instructors would collaborate across the two courses to ensure an overlap in content. This intervention is targeted to all students and promotes students' social cohesion and abilities to make connections across academic disciplines. Descriptive and QE studies have shown connections between learning communities and high levels of student engagement and student persistence. Zachry Rutschow synthesized RCT results from studies at Queensborough Community College and Houston Community College, which indicated that students in learning communities succeeded in developmental mathematics courses at higher rates than their peers; however, these studies have shown moderate effects on the accumulation of mathematics and total academic credits and no positive effect on student persistence. Although learning communities were most popular in 2000, Zachry Rutschow explained that these interventions are not implemented as often as some of the others, given how challenging they are to execute successfully and given the model's limited long-term positive effects. As a result, she continued, there has been a decrease in the number of research studies conducted on this particular intervention.

Self-paced instruction is a type of reform in which course content is separated into short skill-building modules and is often paired with diagnostic assessments. Students typically work independently with an online tutorial or in a computer laboratory with a facilitator. Zachry Rutschow remarked that this reform is targeted to all students and as of 2016 was offered by 40 percent of public 2-year institutions across the United States. This reform has been mandated in Virginia and North Carolina and is now endorsed in Florida, Idaho, and West Virginia. The original intent of this model was to accelerate students' progress through developmental mathematics, given that they only had to complete corresponding modules to strengthen specific skills and could bypass other aspects of the course. However, studies indicate that technology-based instruction can be difficult for both students and educators. Descriptive studies in North Carolina, Tennessee, and Virginia; a QE study in Tennessee; and an RCT study in Texas all showed that students actually tended to *slow* their pace when taking modular courses. Zachry Rutschow surmised that this reform might not be the most effective strategy to accelerate students through developmental mathematics.

Owing to an increase in the number of careers that require statistical and quantitative literacy, the multiple mathematics pathways model has emerged as another type of reform in response to the traditional "algebra-for-all" approach to mathematics education, Zachry Rutschow commented. The multiple mathematics pathways approach aligns mathematics course content directly with students' intended majors and careers (e.g., quantitative literacy for humanities majors, statistics for social and health sciences majors, and calculus for STEM majors), often integrates high-quality instruction, and accelerates students' progress through developmental mathematics. Although this reform was originally targeted toward students with higher-level mathematics skills, it is expanding to target students placed in multiple levels of developmental mathematics. According to Zachry Rutschow, 41 percent of public 2-year institutions offer multiple mathematics pathways—Carnegie's Statway and Quantway programs[6] and the Dana Center Mathematics Pathways (DCMP)[7] are examples of successful programs of this set of reforms, and many states (e.g., California, Indiana, Massachusetts, Michigan, and Texas) have adopted these pathways as part of their policies. Zachry Rutschow described an RCT study of multiple mathematics pathways at CUNY that indicated highly promising results around the completion of college-level mathematics courses as well as the accumulation of credits.

Student Support Reforms

Zachary Rutschow shared that many students with developmental course needs often have limited knowledge of experiences and expectations at the postsecondary level, and described the additional supports that have been implemented to help these students navigate the system of higher

---

[6]For more information about Carnegie's Statway and Quantway programs, see https://carnegiemathpathways.org and Chapter 4 of this proceedings.

[7]For more information about the DCMP program, see https://www.utdanacenter.org/our-work/higher-education/dana-center-mathematics-pathways and Chapters 3 and 4 of this proceedings.

education, build skills, and develop an attachment to college in general. One way, she described, is through success courses (i.e., study skills courses or student orientation courses), and according to a 2009 survey of 1,000 institutions, success courses were offered at 87 percent of 2- and 4-year institutions as either stand-alone courses or in combination with a developmental course. Success courses, she continued, are targeted toward students with multiple developmental education needs, and they have the potential to improve students' psychosocial skills, to increase students' familiarity with their institutions, and to improve students' study skills. Additionally, students can often earn either developmental or college-level course credit upon completion of a success course. A number of studies suggest that success courses lead to positive short-term effects on student persistence, credit accumulation, and grade achievement; however, longer-term studies suggest that these impacts are not sustained over time, she explained.

Zachry Rutschow shared that another way to increase support for developmental education students is by providing tutoring and supplemental instruction (i.e., a peer or instructor is paired with a class and facilitates a separate support section). Tutoring and supplemental instruction initiatives are targeted toward all students, and many postsecondary institutions have established tutoring centers. Additionally, Alaska, California, Colorado, Kentucky, Ohio, and West Virginia all currently encourage supplemental instruction to enhance the success of developmental education students. An RCT study showed that tutoring could achieve modest effects on credit accumulation and persistence for students when paired with other supports. Zachry Rutschow's synthesis also highlighted descriptive studies of supplemental instruction, which indicated increased positive results for students, including higher grades and grade point averages, lower course withdrawal rates, and higher persistence rates.

Intensive advising—more regular interactions with advisers through multiple modes of communication (e.g., in-person meetings, e-mail, phone, text messaging)—is a third way for *all* students to be better supported and informed about important academic deadlines and milestones, Zachry Rutschow explained. To facilitate this high and frequent level of engagement with their students, advisers who participate in intensive advising programs often have reduced advising caseloads. Although intensive advising models can be difficult to scale, the use of technology to facilitate communication between students and their advisers is encouraging, according to Zachry Rutschow's review of the literature. Intensive advising over multiple semesters has been shown in an RCT study to increase student persistence. However, she commented that, in general, when student support reform models have been implemented on their own, they have not shown as many positive effects on academic progress as other reform models or as when used in combination with other reform initiatives.

Comprehensive Reforms

Zachry Rutschow asserted that individual, short-term interventions show fewer positive effects on student success than more comprehensive, long-term interventions. Thus, many academic institutions are taking a more holistic approach to reform that integrates a combination of the previously described strategies in the form of guided pathways or wraparound support models. Unlike the multiple mathematics pathways programs, which focus on course content by aligning mathematics coursework with a student's major or career interest, the guided pathways model emphasizes comprehensive student support by mapping courses for completion, providing strong advising and student supports, offering accelerated developmental courses, delivering early alerts and interventions, and striving for coherent learning outcomes. Targeted to all students, at least 250 postsecondary institutions in 10 states currently have guided pathways programs. Zachry Rutschow's research highlighted the findings of descriptive studies of guided pathways, which indicated that students accumulate more credits faster during their first year in college and have better completion rates in college mathematics and English than students who attended college before the implementation of guided pathways. However, these studies, she continued also specified small decreases in both student persistence rates and overall pass rates in college courses.

The CUNY Accelerated Study in Associate Programs[8] (ASAP) and the CUNY Start Program,[9] Zachry Rutschow explained, are examples of comprehensive reforms that provide wraparound support. CUNY ASAP, she continued, supports full-time students with one or two developmental needs by providing intensive advising, paired courses, a study skills course, and tuition waivers, while CUNY Start focuses on providing comprehensive support to students with low skill levels and three developmental needs. Additionally, Zachry Rutschow shared that students can enroll in the CUNY Start Program full or part time, at a negligible cost, and they receive instruction in reading, writing, and mathematics via a cohort model *prior* to matriculation in college.

Zachry Rutschow noted that these two programs are just beginning to scale and thus are not yet as widespread as guided pathways programs. Nevertheless, preliminary findings from an RCT study of the CUNY Start Program suggest that CUNY Start students are both progressing through developmental courses and enrolling at higher rates after completing the program. Studies of CUNY ASAP have revealed impressive positive results,

---

[8]For more information about CUNY ASAP, see http://www1.cuny.edu/sites/asap and Chapter 5 of this proceedings.

[9]For more information about the CUNY Start Program, see http://www1.cuny.edu/sites/cunystart and the latter part of Chapter 4 of this proceedings.

she explained, with improved student outcomes, increased credit accumulation, and a near doubling of the rate of students graduating with an associate's degree within 3 years.

DISCUSSION

In response to a question from Julie Phelps, professor of mathematics at Valencia College, about research on individual reforms, Zachry Rutschow suggested that intensive (i.e., reforms that change instruction or the sequencing of courses) and comprehensive reforms seem to hold the most potential for improving students' overall academic success. Reflecting on the data presented by Zachry Rutschow, which showed that low-income students and students from underrepresented groups are overrepresented in developmental mathematics, panelist Aditya Adiredja, assistant professor of mathematics education at the University of Arizona, wondered what the data would show if one controlled for race and socioeconomic background in experiments that measure the effectiveness of reforms. Would the recommendations about the most promising approaches remain the same? Zachry Rutschow replied that some of the studies do include subgroup analyses and most disaggregate to evaluate the effects of reforms on closing the achievement gap, and the results have been encouraging. Rebecca Fitch, former project manager for the Civil Rights Data Collection at the U.S. Department of Education, asked if there are any efforts under way to make schools and communities that feed into local 2-year institutions more aware of what students need to do and know to be prepared for college-level mathematics. Zachry Rutschow noted that some states have attempted alignment across K–12 and postsecondary institutions, especially through early assessment programs.

EDUCATIONAL EQUITY AND DEVELOPMENTAL MATHEMATICS REFORM

While the most common reforms in developmental education—assessment and placement, structure and sequence, instruction and content, student support, and comprehensive reforms that embrace one or more of these strategies—have proven successful in some instances, Zachry Rutschow revealed that these reforms are not reaching all students, and even in cases in which the data suggest that the reform approach is successful, some students are still not well served (Zachry Rutschow, 2019). The workshop's panel on educational equity and mathematics reform brought together both educators and leaders from national education initiatives to discuss current inequities in the developmental mathematics landscape as well as strategies to better serve students from underrepresented populations in this era of reform.

Before sharing their perspectives on student equity issues in developmental mathematics education, panelists provided brief overviews of their professional experiences and research interests. Panel moderator James Dorsey, a self-professed "child who could not do math," is the president and chief executive officer of the College Success Foundation,[10] a national education reform program that helps students enroll in and complete college. Previously, Dorsey was executive director and president of Mathematics, Engineering, Science Achievement (MESA)[11]—an almost 50-year-old program started in California that builds pathways to degrees and careers in science, technology, engineering, and mathematics (STEM) for students from backgrounds that are historically underrepresented in mathematics-based fields. This program specifically supports students through success courses, intensive advising, supplemental instruction, and leadership preparation. This successful program has been replicated in several other states, including Florida, Georgia, New York, Texas, and Washington.

Adiredja focuses his research specifically on equity issues in undergraduate mathematics education. As an alumnus of the Professional Development Program at the University of California, Berkeley, he has a particular interest in "how reform efforts serve black and brown students" and how deficit narratives negatively impact classroom interactions—for instance, faculty might treat students in developmental mathematics as though they cannot do mathematics compared to students in calculus, thereby negatively influencing how the mathematical work of students in developmental mathematics is perceived and creating different opportunities for different groups of students.

As the senior project director at the Opportunity Institute,[12] panelist Pamela Burdman reconceptualizes the role of mathematics in education equity with the purpose of informing policy through a project called Just Equations.[13] Similar to Adiredja, Burdman studies the narratives that are told and the assumptions that are made about education that undermine equity and justice. She endorsed the definition of mathematics equity as "the inability to predict mathematics achievement and participation based solely on student characteristics such as race, class, ethnicity, sex, beliefs, and proficiency in the dominant language" (Gutierrez, 2007) and noted that the education system in the United States is far from achieving equity (Burdman, 2018). The architecture of mathematics is built on misconceptions about mathematics learning—in other words, who can and cannot

---

[10]For more information about the College Success Foundation, see https://www.collegesuccessfoundation.org.

[11]For more information about the MESA program, see https://mesausa.org.

[12]For more information about the Opportunity Institute, see https://theopportunityinstitute.org.

[13]For more information about the Just Equations project, see https://justequations.org.

> Mathematics equity: "the inability to predict mathematics achievement and participation based solely on student characteristics such as race, class, ethnicity, sex, beliefs, and proficiency in the dominant language" (Gutierrez, 2007).

learn mathematics and the notion that mathematics is about speed and right or wrong answers. This architecture is also framed by existing educational inequities—mathematics as a gatekeeper, differential access to high quality curriculum and instruction, and teacher biases—which result in negative psychological effects on students, she explained. As a result, women, low-income students, adult learners, and students of color, in particular, are having negative experiences in mathematics. Burdman declared "this is not fair to students ... but it is also really not fair to math," which as a discipline suffers without the inclusion of these groups of students. "It is not the purpose of math to make students' lives difficult, to make them anxious, or to hate math," she asserted. Instead of serving as a means to categorize or discourage students, mathematics could "expand professional opportunities, [be used to] understand and critique the world, and [elicit] wonder, joy, and beauty" (National Council of Teachers of Mathematics, 2019). She emphasized that redesigning the architecture of mathematics to create equitable opportunities requires working across multiple dimensions: content, instruction, assessment, and readiness policies and practices.

Panelist Maxine Roberts is the assistant director of knowledge management for Strong Start to Finish,[14] an initiative of the Education Commission of the States. Strong Start to Finish focuses on developmental education reform with the goals of (1) increasing the number and proportion of students who are placed into and complete gateway mathematics and English within their first year of college and (2) aligning this with a program of study. Strong Start to Finish is also interested in supporting students of color, low-income students, and adult learners. This is achieved in three ways: (1) engaging with systems that are scaling developmental education reforms, (2) supporting a network of institutions that are advancing developmental education in key areas, and (3) deepening knowledge about how reforms are enacted. Roberts is particularly interested in unpacking

---

[14] For more information about Strong Start to Finish, see https://strongstart.org.

the reforms to determine whether there are missing elements that, when added, could substantially improve the student experience. Specifically, in her work, she considers the classroom experiences that African American and Latino students have in developmental education and how this relates to their academic progress. Additionally, she considers how faculty and peer engagement influence the development of students' mathematics identities (i.e., How do they view themselves as mathematics learners and doers?). Roberts explained that "so many times, it is easy to say, well, gosh, these students are not ready, and that is the deficit perspective."

Panelist Joanna Sanchez is a program manager at Excelencia in Education,[15] a nonprofit organization in Washington, DC, whose mission is to accelerate Latino student success in higher education through data, practice, and leadership. Excelencia in Education highlights programs across the United States that have successfully supported Latino students in higher education through its annual "Examples of Excelencia"[16] awards and provides an evidence base of best practices for mathematics education in its "Growing What Works" database.[17] Drawing on her personal experience as a student from the Texas border, she observed that students who are successful in mathematics tend to have access to opportunities that others may not have, which reinforces the need for reforms that eliminate inequitable trajectories for students.

Moving into the moderated question-and-answer portion of the panel, Dorsey asked the panelists to discuss the dominant narrative of success in developmental mathematics reform—which is centered on achievement gap, quantitative data, and race/ethnicity—and to consider how this dominant narrative affects student outcomes. Burdman claimed that the student experience is missing from the dominant narrative. Although quantitative data help to gauge progress, they do not necessarily indicate why and for whom a program is successful. Adiredja suggested taking a few steps back and first evaluating the dominant methods that are used to investigate this issue. He made a distinction between *controlling for race* and *disaggregating data by race* in the research, the latter of which he says leads to the idea of closing the achievement gap. Such discussions, he continued, can then lead to implicit deficit positioning of non-white students to "catch up" to the dominant students (i.e., white and Asian students and certain East Asian students, in particular). Adiredja explained that *controlling for race* instead would allow the focus to shift, prompting the study of particular groups of

---

[15] For more information about Excelencia in Education, see https://www.edexcelencia.org.

[16] For more information about the Examples of Excelencia awards, see https://www.edexcelencia.org/programs-initiatives/examples-excelencia.

[17] For more information on the Growing What Works database, see https://www.edexcelencia.org/programs-initiatives/growing-what-works-database.

students *on their own* and a better understanding of the kinds of reforms that could help these specific students succeed.

Although successful mathematics course completion and subsequent degree completion are important desired outcomes of reform efforts, Dorsey asked panelists to share other ideal reform outcomes that would be relevant to the development of students' identities and career pathways. Roberts hoped that reform efforts could prompt more developmental mathematics students to enroll in STEM-related courses for the sake of general learning (as opposed to *only* for career preparation), while Burdman said it would be ideal for students to develop quantitative literacy in ways that are meaningful for their respective careers and their lives. Sanchez and Adiredja both expressed hope that students would see themselves reflected more often in a diverse professoriate as a result of reform. Adiredja added that although the dominant narrative about the importance of enrolling in STEM courses is informed by aspirations for economic stability, career mobility, and global competitiveness, he simply wished for students to experience the joy of learning mathematics. He stressed that for "the folks who went through the system and succeeded, some carrying the title of 'the first,' we often do not talk about the personal costs it takes to get there … oftentimes that journey to get there is not the most joyful." Thus, Adiredja feels that one of the goals of his work is actually to foster joyful mathematics and STEM learning experiences for students.

Acknowledging the disproportionate representation of certain populations in STEM fields and the specific groups of students who have struggled to succeed in mathematics, Dorsey asked the panelists how mathematics reform could be used as a lever to enhance equity, particularly in STEM fields. Sanchez emphasized that successful programs exist, such as the Emerging Scholars Program, that focus specifically on Latino students' success through postsecondary studies and into the professoriate using a cohort-based model. One program that began in 2005 in the Department of Mathematics at The University of Texas at Austin and incorporated the Emerging Scholars Program is still thriving today and is expanding across the University of Texas system. Taking a different approach to Dorsey's question, Adiredja described the "status that is conferred to people who know mathematics" and championed the value of helping students to develop the "mathematical efficiency" to be able to participate rather than be shut out of conversations among people with mathematical understanding.

Referencing a conversation that took place among the panelists prior to the panel discussion, Adiredja noted that Dorsey himself benefitted from a self-paced mathematics course, even though it was not a "recommended" approach based on the research shared by Zachry Rutschow, which indicated that this approach tended to slow student progress. Adiredja described Dorsey's experience as one that could be inaccurately interpreted as "statistical noise" in student data. When looking at student data as a whole instead of thinking about students' individual experiences, he continued, opportunities to serve students, especially those in underrepresented populations, are missed. To enhance equity, Roberts suggested that the mathematics education community should first consider the dominant perspective of "success" and whether students are excluded if they do not fit precisely in that definition. She referred to a conversation she had with several African American students who defined success not as the receipt of a passing grade but rather as the ability to explain mathematical concepts to people in an understandable way. Roberts underscored the need to look closely at the groups of students that comprise developmental education and "tap into the knowledge" that they have; redefining "success" will broaden the pool of students who view themselves as successful and are recognized as successful.

Dorsey shared a personal experience from 1984 when he approached the Mathematics Department at Chico State University about adding a supplemental instruction component to precalculus and algebra courses to better support students' goals of attaining degrees in engineering. The chair of the department initially resisted the idea because "he had only seen one African-American [student] pass a calculus course in 8 years." However, after a class of six students of color passed the precalculus course, as well as the calculus course that followed, the department chair reversed his decision and approved the development of a cohort for students of color. Today, Dorsey announced, there are 34 cohorts of these students of color who earned degrees in mathematics, physics, and chemistry. This experience illustrates the importance of developing relationships across academic departments—in this case, between the Mathematics Department, which usually acts as a gatekeeper, and the College of Engineering—to align mathematics experiences with career pathways and to provide underrepresented populations with the tools to succeed in STEM.

Building on Zachry Rutschow's presentation about reforms in developmental mathematics education, Dorsey asked panelists if the ideal outcomes that they outlined are in fact attainable by way of the current assessment, placement, and instructional reforms. Roberts pointed out that reforming structure is only part of the way to achieve student success. Students' experiences have to be changed too, she continued, and a focus has to be placed on enhancing students' identities as mathematics learners and doers (see Aguirre, Mayfield-Ingram, and Martin, 2013). These more positive experiences and practices can carry forward in students who choose to become mathematics instructors in the future. Burdman accentuated the need for institutions to provide more support to students to enable them to develop agency to make authentic choices about which mathematics pathways they follow. This will help to keep the implementation of reforms aligned with the intention of the reforms, she continued, which is to promote student success in STEM rather than divert students away from STEM based on deficit assumptions of their ability. In line with this, Adiredja noted that in addition to implementing assessment, placement, and instructional reforms, it is essential for faculty to develop growth mindsets of ability. These mindsets should not be "filtered through the lens of race" (i.e., affording more growth mindset to certain students compared to others) so as to avoid negatively impacting specific groups of students. He also expressed the urgent need for reform efforts to extend further to engage with racism, sexism, and ableism dimensions.

Panelists invited members of the audience to share their questions and observations about equity issues in developmental mathematics education. Citing Adiredja's desire for students to find the joy in mathematics, online participant Sandra Byrd, who teaches at a tribal college, pointed out that "mathematics is excruciatingly painful" for some students. "Getting the students to find joy and success in math is a hard journey," she continued. "Some of the teachers in the past have made math painful for these students, and it makes the students reluctant to approach math, to ask for help and to receive help when it is offered, and to persevere." Roberts agreed with Byrd's reflections and emphasized that faculty perceptions of their students have strong impacts on whether students view themselves with the potential to be successful. When "students of color, low-income students, and adult learners enter a math classroom, it is not just about learning content; it is about learning how to navigate environments that can be treacherous…and [psychologically] violent," Roberts asserted. She described conversations with successful students who "cried as they talked about their math experiences and the struggles they had." Thus, a balance between structural reform and the reform of relational practices is crucial, she proclaimed. Adiredja agreed that "math is [psychologically] violent" for students, but also cautioned against the tendency to respond from a deficit framework, emphasizing that lowering expectations is not the solution to addressing students' mathematics trauma.

Struck by Adiredja's earlier comment about one person's noise being another person's signal, Mark Green declared that it is time to look at students individually, both in terms of their backgrounds and their unique learning styles. He asked panelists about the potential role of cultural competency training for developmental mathematics faculty. Although developing true cultural competence is difficult, Adiredja steered participants to resources from the K–12 domain on developing culturally inclusive pedagogy. He encouraged faculty to consider "how they view their students [and whether they are] mindful of their own sort of racial and gender biases in interpreting students' work." To illuminate this suggestion, Adiredja described watching a video of his own teaching, in which he saw himself "walking into a group of students [one Latino student, one Latina student, and one white female student] ... and talking to the two women, but [his] back the whole time was against the one Latino male student ... [about whom] the department [has] an established narrative ... because he is taking more time, he has not graduated in 5 years, and he is struggling in the program." Adiredja emphasized that his action was subconscious; despite his extensive research in deficit narratives, he did not realize that "at that moment ... [he had] shut down that opportunity" for a student who was also dealing with mental health issues. The best way for faculty to counteract these narratives, and the resulting negative impacts on students, is to create an open dialogue with individual students to understand their needs and their experiences, Adiredja advocated.

Vilma Mesa observed that this conversation on equity should include an understanding of not only what works for whom but also under what conditions. She revealed that the mathematics education community is not "counting" certain groups of students—for example, students with disabilities, first-generation college students, Native American students, Middle Eastern students, and Pacific Islander students. "By not counting these groups, we are rendering our ideology about who counts" in the education system, she asserted. Mesa explained that strategies are needed to understand how to attribute the loss of these underrepresented students from mathematics programs, and asked panelists to share examples of promising models for change that could mitigate these losses. In response, Sanchez described an intensive 1-week success course[18] that Latino students at Cañada College take three times per year to become more successful in mathematics, as well as in a number of other disciplines. Dorsey reiterated the value of the MESA program, particularly at El Camino College in California, in supporting underrepresented students, including first-generation students, Native Americans, and Pacific Islanders, to be successful in mathematics. Echoing a previous suggestion from Adiredja, Burdman said that postsecondary educators could learn how to better support populations of students who are not being well served by studying the abundant research on reforms in K–12 mathematics education.

In closing this discussion, Treisman revisited the reforms of the 1970s and 1980s, which were implemented in response to previous reforms focused on student deficits. These new reforms were organized around student assets and focused on producing professionals instead of merely eliminating the achievement gap and helping students to avoid failure. Concentrating research on understanding whether reforms are organized around student deficits or student assets could help to explain differential outcomes of programs that may appear structurally similar, he suggested. Alluding to

---

[18] For more information about this program, see https://canadacollege.edu/jam/mathjam.php.

Zachry Rutschow's observation that new normative structures are being implemented throughout higher education, Treisman pointed out that because it is impossible to retrofit equity to systems that were not designed for it, the hope for equity lies in the space created by these new approaches to "[design] with care about who the beneficiaries are likely to be."

3

Developmental Mathematics Students and Their Experiences

As part of the guiding questions for the workshop, Howard Gobstein shared that in order to make continual improvements to provide equitable learning opportunities to all students and increase their chances of success, it is essential to understand who is enrolled in developmental mathematics, which approaches work for whom, and who is still being left behind. In light of these questions, workshop participants considered data on student demographics and methods to measure student outcomes that together highlight which of the reforms discussed in Chapter 2 are yielding better results for specific subpopulations of students. Additionally, workshop presenters and participants discussed pre- and postreform data on the characteristics of developmental mathematics students and their experiences, from both national and state-level datasets, as a way to better understand how reforms could enhance outcomes for *all* students, to assess if progress has been made, and to determine what additional research might be needed.

UNDERSTANDING THE DEVELOPMENTAL MATHEMATICS STUDENT POPULATION

Michelle Hodara, a manager of research and evaluation at Education Northwest, provided an overview of "Understanding the Developmental Mathematics Student Population: Findings from a Nationally Representative Sample of First-Time College Entrants,"[1] a paper commissioned by the

---

[1] To read Hodara's commissioned paper, see http://sites.nationalacademies.org/cs/groups/dbassesite/documents/webpage/dbasse_191821.pdf.

workshop planning committee; this paper highlights the characteristics of developmental mathematics students nationwide across institution types. She explained that her research was motivated by a series of questions from the workshop planning committee:

- How many students take developmental mathematics at 2- and 4-year institutions?
- What is known about these students?
- Has the population changed over the past decade?
- How can we better characterize this population of students?

She noted that because limited data are currently available, these are difficult questions to answer; as a result, this study should be considered as just the beginning of a research agenda to understand developmental mathematics students in the United States.

Hodara's study was informed by two datasets from the Beginning Postsecondary Students (BPS) Longitudinal Study,[2] which is the only national dataset that contains information about developmental education enrollment patterns, among other student data. The first dataset focused on first-time college entrants (n = 16,684) across 2- and 4-year institutions in 2003–2004. These students were interviewed in 2004, 2006, and 2009, and their course transcripts were collected. The second dataset concentrated on first-time college entrants (n = 24,766) across 2- and 4-year institutions in 2011–2012 (see Table 3-1 for the demographic characteristics of students in this cohort). These students were interviewed in 2012 and 2014, but no course transcripts were collected. The 2011–2012 dataset is thus limited to students' self-reported data, which presents three limitations in the research findings: (1) students could have neglected to report taking developmental education courses; (2) certain groups of students could have been less likely to report their enrollment in developmental courses; and (3) some students may not have enrolled in developmental courses until their second year of college. As Hodara explained in her research, "We may not have a complete picture of the full population of developmental mathematics students in the 2011–2012 cohort. Nevertheless, there is still much to learn from this BPS dataset about the developmental mathematics student population, despite these limitations" (Hodara, 2019).

---

[2] The BPS Longitudinal Study was conducted by the U.S. Department of Education at the National Center for Education Statistics and is a nationally representative sample drawn from the National Postsecondary Student Aid Study. This includes students' background characteristics, levels of high school preparation, college experiences, financial aid data, and postsecondary outcomes.

TABLE 3-1 Demographic Characteristics of Students Who Entered Public 2- and 4-Year Institutions in 2011–2012 and Took Developmental Mathematics (in percentage)

	Public 2-Year	Public 4-Year
Female	58	61
Student of Color	51	56
First Learned to Speak a Language Other Than English	19	19.5
Foreign Born or Had Foreign-Born Parents	28	32
Parents Whose Highest Degree Was a High School Diploma or Less	47	34
Pell Grant Recipient	70	63

SOURCE: Adapted from Hodara (2019).

Because the most recent available data are from 2011–2012, which was an early year of developmental mathematics education reform, this analysis serves as a "baseline picture of the developmental mathematics student population" (see Box 3-1). She asserted that more research is needed to understand the student population being served by the new models of developmental education. Hodara found that across "all institution types, 42 percent of students who started college in 2003–2004 took developmental mathematics." The largest proportions were enrolled at public 2-year institutions and private nonprofit 2-year institutions. By 2011–2012, this rate had not changed substantially, except for an increase at private for-profit 4-year institutions and public 2-year institutions. She noted that the for-profit 4-year sector grew more than 200 percent during this time period, which might explain the increase at these institution types. She presented demographic characteristics of students who entered public 2-year institutions and public 4-year institutions in 2011–2012 and took developmental mathematics, emphasizing that a very diverse group of students is reflected in these populations (refer to Table 3-1).

Hodara observed that the developmental mathematics students in the 2011–2012 cohort were more likely to be female, from historically underrepresented groups, first-generation college students, and Pell Grant recipients compared to their peers in the same institution type who did not take developmental education in their first year of college (see Figure 3-1). She also found that developmental mathematics students in the 2011–2012 cohort were more likely to be from historically underrepresented groups, first-generation college students, and Pell Grant recipients, in addition to being foreign born or having foreign-born parents and first speaking a language other than English, compared to the developmental mathematics

> **BOX 3-1**
> **An Overview of Developmental Mathematics Students from the Beginning Postsecondary Students Longitudinal Study**
>
> - The majority of developmental mathematics students are from historically underrepresented groups.
> - The developmental mathematics population has become more diverse over time, composed of higher proportions of students from historically underrepresented groups.
> - There are larger differences between developmental mathematics students and students who did not take developmental education at public 4-year institutions than at public 2-year institutions.
> - American Indian/Alaska Native, Black/African American, Hispanic/Latino, Native Hawaiian/Pacific Islander students and students who received Pell Grants at 4-year institutions are overrepresented in the developmental mathematics population.
> - Overrepresentation for students of color and low-income students is more problematic at public 4-year institutions than at public 2-year institutions.
> - Among 4-year institution students who passed Algebra 2 or higher in high school, developmental mathematics enrollment rates are highest for American Indian/Alaska Native and lowest for white students and students who did not receive Pell Grants.
> - Among 2-year institution students who passed Algebra 2 or higher in high school, developmental mathematics enrollment rates are highest for Black/African American students and lowest for Native Hawaiian/Pacific Islander students.
>
> SOURCE: Adapted from Hodara (2019).

students in the 2003–2004 cohort (see Figure 3-2). The 2003–2004 cohort was slightly more likely to be female compared to the 2011–2012 cohort.

Using a composition index, Hodara evaluated how the percentage of students in a particular group within the developmental mathematics population compares to the percentage of that particular group in the overall population. This standard measure can reveal the extent to which even small populations are overrepresented in developmental mathematics—for example, a higher proportion of American Indian/Alaska Native students was enrolled in developmental mathematics than was represented in the overall college student population in 2011–2012 (see Figure 3-3). Hodara noted that "overrepresentation for students of color and low-income students is more problematic at 4-year public colleges than 2-year public colleges" (refer to Box 3-1 and Figure 3-3). She suggested that the issue of overrepresentation of students of color and low-income students in

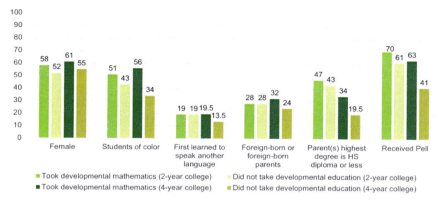

FIGURE 3-1 Profile of students in the 2011–2012 cohort who took developmental mathematics as compared to students who did not take developmental education in the first year of college, by first institution type.
SOURCE: Hodara (2019, slide 10).

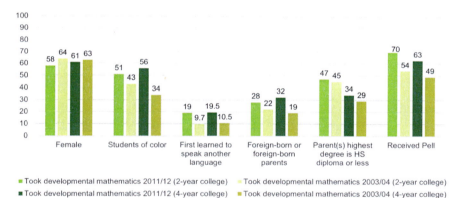

FIGURE 3-2 Profile of students who took developmental mathematics in the 2003–2004 cohort as compared to students who took developmental mathematics in the 2011–2012 cohort, by first institution type.
SOURCE: Hodara (2019, slide 11).

developmental mathematics should prompt critical thought and action from both researchers and educators.

To delve deeper into these questions about overrepresentation, Hodara examined the proportion of students from each racial/ethnic group who took developmental mathematics and had the same level of college readiness. In her analysis, she defined college readiness in the same way that it would be defined based on new multiple measures assessment policies:

36   INCREASING STUDENT SUCCESS IN DEVELOPMENTAL MATHEMATICS

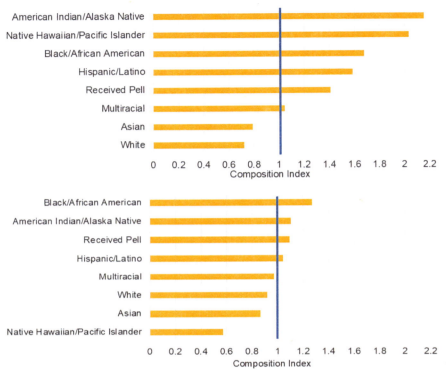

FIGURE 3-3 (top) Representation in developmental mathematics for each racial/ethnic group and students who received Pell Grants at public 4-year institutions in the 2011–2012 cohort and (bottom) representation in developmental mathematics for each racial/ethnic group and students who received Pell Grants at public 2-year institutions in the 2011–2012 cohort.
SOURCE: Hodara (2019, slides 14 and 15).

students are considered college ready if they (1) completed Algebra 2 or higher in high school and (2) had a 2.6 high school grade point average (GPA) (the equivalent of a B–) or higher. Although percentages within each racial/ethnic group varied, she found that overall, 68 percent of the developmental mathematics population in the 2011–2012 cohort completed Algebra 2 in high school and 55 percent had a B– or higher GPA across public 2- and 4-year institutions. Given that these features reflect actual preparedness for college, Hodara was surprised that students with this level of preparation were a part of the developmental mathematics population.

Hodara's additional analyses of student outcomes reflected in the BPS datasets revealed that across all institution types, developmental mathematics students were 3 percentage points more likely to report a decline in mental health from 2012–2014 than students who did not take developmental education during their first year. Developmental mathematics students left their science, technology, engineering, and mathematics (STEM) majors at higher rates than students who did not take developmental education in their first year. Because the relationships between mental health and developmental mathematics and between STEM persistence and developmental mathematics are understudied, it can be difficult to understand how to best address the challenges students experience in their efforts to complete college. Developmental mathematics students were generally less likely to have attained a degree and/or still be enrolled in college after 3 years than students who did not take developmental education in the first year; however, in order to make any significant conclusions about persistence and attainment, students would need to be tracked for much longer than 3 years, she explained.

Hodara concluded with three suggested areas for future research in developmental mathematics education:

1. Developmental mathematics enrollment rates in current models and over time.
2. Characteristics of developmental mathematics student populations in new models.
3. Qualitative and quantitative research on students, especially those in developmental mathematics in the 4-year sector.

She also suggested that causal research should disaggregate impacts by race and ethnicity and other student categories to understand for whom certain reform models are working.

DISCUSSION

Discussion moderator Tatiana Melguizo, associate professor in the Rossier School of Education at the University of Southern California, highlighted the connections between Hodara's research and the importance of the multiple measures assessments previously described by Elizabeth Zachry Rutschow (see Chapter 2). Observing that the data appeared to suggest that community colleges have more rigorous placement requirements than 4-year institutions, Melguizo and Linda Braddy championed Hodara's suggestion to expand research in the 4-year sector. As one possible explanation of these data, Hodara referenced a pre-reform era paper by Fields and Parsad (2012). Their research included a national survey of placement scores across the United States, which showed cutoffs to be higher at 2-year institutions than 4-year institutions—that is, a student with the same score could more likely be placed in developmental mathematics at a 2-year institution than at a 4-year institution. Melguizo noted that California is working to eliminate this issue by setting standards for validating the knowledge that students accumulate in high school. She encouraged using multiple measures assessments more often at 4-year institutions as well as "thinking about how to change the mindsets of the mathematics faculty who are implementing these incredible reforms but might not have kept pace with all of the work from the pathways and the way that the field has been trying to move and shift the way they think about math." Cammie Newmyer, 2018–2019 Albert Einstein Distinguished Educator Fellow, highlighted Colorado's work to standardize community college programs so that the coursework is transferable to universities throughout the state, which, she argued, demonstrates the commitment to rigor in the community college space. Tristan Denley, executive vice chancellor for academic affairs and chief academic officer at the University System of Georgia, noted that around 2011–2012 many states declared that students in 4-year settings were not allowed to be in developmental mathematics, which could heighten misunderstandings of rigor as it relates to mathematics placement requirements.

Philip Uri Treisman pointed out that some of the students in the 2011–2012 BPS cohort might have enrolled in college as a result of the high unemployment rate in the United States—these students would have been older and had more time lapse since they took Algebra 2 than members of the 2003–2004 cohort. Performing an age disaggregation to better understand similarities and differences between the 2003–2004 cohort and the 2011–2012 cohort, he continued, could help academic institutions understand how to better serve students who might be drawn back into higher education during recessions, especially with the anticipation of another recession. Mary Heiss, senior vice president of academic and student affairs at the American Association of Community Colleges, seconded Treisman's suggestion and added that 51 percent of community college students are under age 21, 39 percent are between the ages of 22 and 39, and 10 percent are over age 40. Hodara noted that the students in the cohorts of the BPS study were, on average, age 19 at public 4-year institutions and age 21 at public 2-year institutions, which might be lower ages than what institutions have experienced. Amy Kerwin, vice president of education philanthropy at Ascendium Education Group, advocated for an additional research area that focuses on best serving students who are *not* first-time entrants, especially if the main reason they withdrew is because they were unsuccessful in fulfilling the mathematics requirement. These students could be described as having some college education but no degree, and thus they represent a separate cohort of students that is worthy of examination, she continued.

John Hetts, senior director of data science at the Educational Results Partnership, highlighted the challenges of understanding overrepresentation on campuses where the general population is predominantly composed of students of color (e.g., community colleges), whose placement into developmental mathematics "sets the standard" for these institutions. In response, Hodara advised institutions to think carefully about their individual equity goals when using the composition index as a measure to understand overrepresentation. Aditya Adiredja pointed out that Hodara's data on college readiness challenges the traditional narrative that students are arriving to campus unprepared and refocuses the problem on the structural and policy issues at play. He also wondered if it would be possible to "conceptualize the problem a little bit differently and focus on the students who made it through or the students who persisted" and understand the characteristics of these students. Heidi Schweingruber, director of the Board on Science Education at the National Academies, suggested that if 43 percent of students are beginning college in developmental mathematics, then the definition of college-level mathematics might need to be revisited. "As an educator," she continued, "my philosophy is you meet students where they are and you create opportunities for them to learn and move forward. So it just opens up this whole philosophical question for me about what we are doing." Denley echoed this point and added that many students have overcome considerable obstacles just to attend college, only to be given the message that they are not "college material." Because this impacts the way that students then view their experiences as they progress through developmental education, it is an important issue for the mathematics education community to consider, he continued.

EXPERIENCES FROM FOUR DIFFERENT STATE CONTEXTS

Susan Bickerstaff, senior research associate at the Community College Research Center and panel moderator, introduced the next panel, in which participants explored in greater depth the questions around student outcomes posed during Hodara's presentation, using data from particular state contexts. Bickerstaff reiterated that change in the developmental and introductory mathematics education space is happening quickly, national data are limited, and reforms have differential outcomes for students. Four panelists, each of whom is doing research on developmental mathematics reform in diverse state contexts with various populations of students, shared their findings.[3]

---

[3]Background resources on these presentations can be found at https://sites.nationalacademies.org/DBASSE/BOSE/devmathhandouts/index.htm.

Student Preparation and Developmental Mathematics in Tennessee

Angela Boatman, assistant professor of public policy and higher education in the Department of Leadership, Policy, and Organizations at Vanderbilt University, shared research on the relationship between student preparation and success in developmental mathematics in Tennessee. Boatman discussed the differential impacts of developmental mathematics, focusing specifically on students with the lowest standardized test scores in the state of Tennessee, and whether impacts on these students vary by instructional method. Standardized tests are commonly used for efficient placement, becoming the gatekeeper to college-level mathematics. However, these exams are noisy measures of students' abilities, and high degrees of variation exist in what is considered "remedial" across institutions in Tennessee. Remediated students often have no better, and sometimes worse, outcomes than their peers who are placed directly into college-level courses, according to Boatman.

Boatman explained that prior to the era of reform in Tennessee, approximately 19 percent of students with a score of 18 on the mathematics section of the ACT and entering community college in Fall 2012 passed college mathematics in their first three semesters. Students in that same cohort with a score of 13 on the mathematics section of the ACT passed college mathematics in the first three semesters at a rate of only 5 percent. After a series of reforms were implemented (e.g., the co-requisite model), approximately 25 percent of students with a score of 18 on the mathematics section of the ACT and entering community college in Fall 2014 passed college mathematics in their first three semesters. However, students with a score of 13 on the mathematics section of the ACT still only passed college mathematics in their first three semesters at a rate of 5 percent. When the lowest-scoring students were placed into basic mathematics courses prior to the initial implementation of reforms, she continued, they passed college mathematics within 2 years at a rate of only 8 percent, which raises questions about the value of developmental mathematics for all student groups (see Figure 3-4).

Boatman shared competing hypotheses for how low-scoring students might be harmed or could benefit from developmental mathematics courses: (1) multiple developmental mathematics course sequences slow student progress, which could lead to lower self-esteem, higher frustration, and higher drop-out rates, as well as more time and money needed to complete college (although the effect may not be as prominent at colleges where the majority of peers have similar levels of preparedness) or (2) basic, foundational skills taught in lower-level developmental mathematics courses could be more beneficial for student success in subsequent college courses

DEVELOPMENTAL MATHEMATICS STUDENTS AND THEIR EXPERIENCES   41

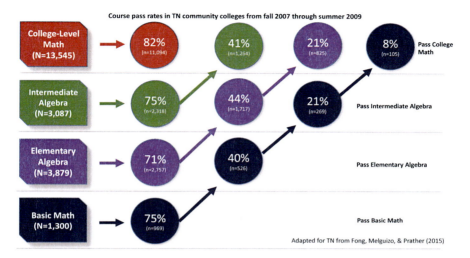

FIGURE 3-4 Mathematics course pass rates prior to the era of reform in Tennessee community colleges from Fall 2007 through Summer 2009, illustrating Boatman's finding that developmental mathematics does not positively impact student outcomes (compared to students directly placed into college-level mathematics).
SOURCES: Boatman (2019, slide 6); data from Tennessee Board of Regents.

compared to the lessons taught in courses just below college level, and thus community colleges might focus more supports on students placed in these lower-level courses.

Additionally, Boatman shared findings from a study by Xu and Dadgar (2018) across 23 community colleges in Virginia, which revealed that when assigned to three rather than two remedial mathematics courses, students experienced no benefit for completing a college-level mathematics course or an associate's degree. The study also showed that students at the lowest levels of academic preparedness would have also benefitted from skipping the third remedial mathematics course. Boatman and Long (2018) studied 13 community colleges in Tennessee and found that the largest negative effects on college completion occurred among students who needed and were assigned to only one developmental mathematics course. In alignment with these findings, eliminating the higher-level developmental mathematics course and placing students directly into college-level mathematics led to greater success for students in both Tennessee and Virginia. For students with the lowest scores (i.e., below 16 on the mathematics section of the ACT), they observed small positive effects (e.g., increases in degree or certificate completion) over a long period of time. The key takeaways from both studies, Boatman explained, are that developmental education students are not a homogeneous group and developmental courses affect students differently depending on their levels of academic preparedness.

To address issues of college readiness, the Tennessee Seamless Alignment and Integrated Learning Support (SAILS) Program was created in 2013. This early assessment program affords the completion of a college developmental mathematics course during a student's senior year of high school. This online program is modular and self-paced, delivering all of the content while teachers serve more as tutors. An evaluation of some of the early SAILS cohorts showed generally positive effects in earning college credits and passing college-level mathematics after taking the SAILS course, and those effects were driven by the lowest-scoring students. Boatman also described the Emporium model, another online program that is similar to the SAILS program except that the developmental course is taken in college instead of in high school. Concerns remain about self-paced online learning, and researchers continue to investigate its value. For example, Xu and Jaggars (2014) found that, in general, students with lower GPAs tended to perform worse in courses that are offered online or are technology driven. Similarly, in a study looking at the adoption of the Emporium model across the state of Tennessee, Boatman has so far seen more negative outcomes for the lowest-scoring students, older students, and Pell Grant recipients, as well as more negative effects for students in 2-year institutions. This suggests that online, self-paced learning might not be the best approach in the college setting, which aligns with the findings presented by Zachry Rutschow (see Chapter 2). Boatman reiterated that more research needs to be conducted on the range of the academic needs of students in developmental mathematics, and that it is important for students to develop fundamental skills, but it is equally important not to delay their progress to college completion.

Reform for Developmental Mathematics Requirements in Florida

Toby Park-Gaghan, associate professor of economics of education and education policy and associate director of the Center for Postsecondary Success at Florida State University,[4] shared his research on student outcomes pre- and postreform of developmental education enrollment requirements in Florida. Park-Gaghan discussed the path to eliminating developmental mathematics requirements in the state of Florida through a statewide

---

[4]The Center for Postsecondary Success (CPS) is a research center dedicated to identifying and evaluating institutional, state, and federal policies and programs that may serve to improve student success. CPS provides support for, and fosters collaboration, among those who are interested in conducting research on student success in postsecondary education. For more information on CPS, see http://centerforpostsecondarysuccess.org.

initiative. Florida Senate Bill 1720,[5] implemented in Fall 2014, made placement tests optional and created an exempt student category, which gave those students the option to bypass developmental education and enroll directly into college-level coursework. Exempt students include students who entered a Florida high school in 2003 (or later) and graduated with a standard diploma, as well as active-duty members of the U.S. Armed Services. This bill also changed the way that Florida postsecondary institutions taught developmental education, with the implementation of co-requisite and compression models.

Using a comparative interrupted time series and data on cohorts of first-time-in-college students from the Florida Department of Education's longitudinal record system, Park-Gaghan and his team explored how removing the "roadblock" of developmental education, especially for students of traditionally underrepresented races and ethnicities, would impact student success (Hu et al., 2019). Ultimately, they wanted to understand whether more students were successfully enrolling in and passing gateway mathematics courses (i.e., college-level courses required to pass for a program of study) as a direct result of Florida Senate Bill 1720. Starting with the 2014 cohort of students, a significant and positive increase was apparent in the number of students enrolled in gateway mathematics courses; additionally, black and Hispanic students were enrolling at faster rates in these courses than their white counterparts. Even with increased enrollment rates, course-based passing rates—the share of students enrolled in the courses who passed the class—remained similar to what they were previously except for black students, who experienced a slight decrease in passing rates.

While not all students who chose to enroll in gateway courses were successful in passing the course, cohort-based passing rates—the share of incoming students who passed a gateway mathematics course—increased since the implementation of Florida Senate Bill 1720, with black and Hispanic students having greater gains than white students, Park-Gaghan explained. Thus, overall achievement has been raised for everyone and, in some cases, even more so for black and Hispanic students. All of these findings suggest that Florida Senate Bill 1720 is having a consistent, substantive, and positive impact on student success; the reform seems to have helped to mitigate the performance gap between white and underrepresented students, contributing to equalizing postsecondary educational outcomes. Furthermore, Park-Gaghan explained, the regression-adjusted analyses substantiate that the changes observed pre- and postreform are not occurring purely due to random chance. Implications for practice, he continued, include redefining

---

[5]For more information on Florida Senate Bill 1720, see https://www.flsenate.gov/Session/Bill/2013/1720.

who is required to take developmental education and how it is taught, which requires attention to both the instructional practices and the structure of college-level courses. Additionally, he asserted that increased advising and enhanced student support services are integral parts of developmental education reform and overall student success. He concluded by emphasizing that research could play an important role in informing policy related to the implementation of developmental mathematics reforms (e.g., how to redesign mathematics pathways and revise institutional approaches to course offerings).

Assessment and Placement Reform in California

Hetts discussed the implementation of assessment and placement reform in California and its impacts on student outcomes. He observed that when students move from the K–12 system to the community college system in California, approximately 75 percent have to repeat one or more courses that they successfully completed in high school. That impact falls disproportionately on people of color, women (specifically in the case of mathematics), and low-income students. Approved in 2017, California Law AB-705[6] requires educational institutions to justify their decisions about who is placed into a developmental education pathway: students have to be highly unlikely to succeed in a college-level course, and the institution has to demonstrate that placing them into a developmental mathematics sequence will increase their likelihood of completing a college-level mathematics course. In light of this new policy and given the fact that so many students are repeating courses that they already successfully completed in high school, educational leaders have been inspired to identify a new method for placing students into courses.

The Multiple Measures Assessment Project[7] is an ongoing, collaborative effort of the California Community Colleges Chancellor's Office, Common Assessment Initiative, Cal-Partnership for Achieving Student Success Plus, the RP Group, and more than 90 pilot community colleges in California to assess and place students more accurately into mathematics and English sequences—not only in developmental education but also in courses such as calculus and Calculus 2. The multiple measures data that are identified, analyzed, and validated include students' high school transcript data, non-cognitive variable data (e.g., students' motivation or perceptions of their own skill levels), and self-reported high school transcript data.

---

[6]For more information about California AB-705, see https://leginfo.legislature.ca.gov/faces/billNavClient.xhtml?bill_id=201720180AB705.
[7]For more information about the Multiple Measures Assessment Project, see https://rpgroup.org/All-Projects/ArticleView/articleId/118.

> "Approved in 2017, California Law AB-705 requires educational institutions to justify their decisions about who is placed into a developmental education pathway: students have to be highly unlikely to succeed in a college-level course, and the institution has to demonstrate that placing them into a developmental mathematics sequence will increase their likelihood of completing a college-level mathematics course."

Hetts explained that results from an analysis to predict course success indicated that students with a high school GPA greater than 3.0 (or students with a slightly lower GPA but who progressed further in mathematics) are likely to succeed in courses such as statistics if they begin at the level of college statistics. Students with a GPA of 3.4 or higher and at least Algebra 2 (or with a slightly lower GPA and successful completion of calculus in high school) are likely to succeed in precalculus if they begin at the level of precalculus. However, historically, only 15 percent of students in the California community colleges were placed directly into a college-level mathematics course. Using these new standards for multiple measures assessments, he estimated that 40 percent of students could be placed directly into college-level courses and thus given a better opportunity to succeed.

Students in the Multiple Measures Assessment pilot programs completed college courses at a rate of 67 percent, which is the same rate of success as students with traditional placement into college-level courses. In comparison, students at these same colleges who started one level below college-level mathematics succeeded at a rate of 27 percent, and students who started two levels below succeeded at a rate of 16 percent. Multiple measures assessments have helped to identify students who are most likely to succeed, yet 60 percent of students are still not included in that category. Looking more closely at this remaining population of students who would be described as "least likely to succeed," and employing the analysis used to predict course success, Hetts observed that their success rates in a college-level mathematics course is approximately 40 percent (MMAP Team, 2018; see Figure 3-5). However, if these same students start just one level below college-level mathematics, only 10 to 15 percent of them are successful.

46 INCREASING STUDENT SUCCESS IN DEVELOPMENTAL MATHEMATICS

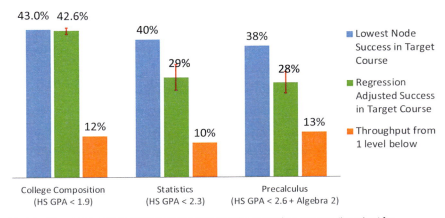

CA statewide success rates in first attempt at college level (no support) vs. one year throughput for students least likely to succeed in course.(error bars represent ±1 se)

FIGURE 3-5 Even the lowest-performing high school students are more likely to complete college-level mathematics successfully if placed directly into a college-level mathematics course.
SOURCE: Modified from MMAP Team (2018).

Taken together, he continued, these findings illustrate that placement leads to differential outcomes for students in terms of the completion of college-level mathematics. Furthermore, all students essentially benefit from a pathway that starts at the college level, and these patterns hold across (1) race/ethnicity, (2) gender, (3) Extended Opportunity Programs and Services status, (4) Disabled Student Programs and Services status, (5) English language learner status, and (6) Pell Grant eligibility, he continued.

Initial data from a selection of California community colleges on student success rates in an open-access co-requisite statistics course by GPA band show that high school GPA is indeed highly predictive of performance. Students at the lowest level of performance (as defined by high school GPA) who start in this gateway college-level mathematics course with supports can complete it successfully 50–60 percent of the time. Without the support, the success rate might have been 30 percent, and starting at just one level below might have reduced the completion rate to 10 percent. "College-level mathematics is for everyone," Hetts reiterated, and the next step is to determine how to best support all students in the appropriate mathematics classes.

Student Access to Reform in Texas

Lauren Schudde, assistant professor in the Department of Educational Leadership and Policy at The University of Texas at Austin, shared her

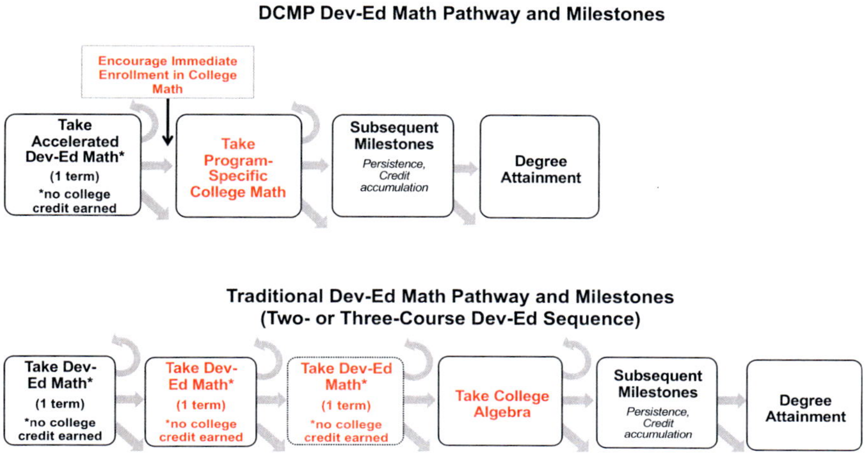

DCMP Dev-Ed Math Pathway and Milestones

[Flowchart: Take Accelerated Dev-Ed Math* (1 term) *no college credit earned → Take Program-Specific College Math → Subsequent Milestones: Persistence, Credit accumulation → Degree Attainment. Above: Encourage Immediate Enrollment in College Math]

Traditional Dev-Ed Math Pathway and Milestones
(Two- or Three-Course Dev-Ed Sequence)

[Flowchart: Take Dev-Ed Math* (1 term) *no college credit earned → Take Dev-Ed Math* (1 term) *no college credit earned → Take Dev-Ed Math* (1 term) *no college credit earned → Take College Algebra → Subsequent Milestones: Persistence, Credit accumulation → Degree Attainment]

FIGURE 3-6 The DCMP model and milestones in contrast to a traditional developmental mathematics education pathway and milestones.
SOURCE: Modified from Schudde and Keisler (2019).

findings on student access to new approaches to developmental mathematics education in the state of Texas. She observed that although much reform is under way, it is not being done fully at scale (i.e., some colleges roll out the reformed models while still primarily offering traditional developmental mathematics sequences) and many students are being left behind.

Schudde's discussion focused on the Dana Center Mathematics Pathways (DCMP) model,[8] a model that combines the structural reform of developmental mathematics education with curricular and advising reform into pathways that offer students field-specific college mathematics. It includes a one-term accelerated developmental education course (noncredit bearing) paired with an optional success course that prepares students for college-level mathematics, including statistics, quantitative reasoning, and algebra courses. Additionally, this model encourages immediate enrollment in college-level mathematics upon passing the developmental mathematics course, uses student-centered approaches and real-world examples to teach mathematics concepts, and is dramatically shorter in duration than a traditional developmental mathematics pathway (see Figure 3-6).

To understand who participates in DCMP (compared to traditional developmental mathematics education) as well as the outcomes associated with this model, Schudde evaluated statewide student-level longitudinal

---

[8]For more information on the DCMP model, see https://dcmathpathways.org.

data in Texas from Fall 2014, 2015, and 2016. For this presentation, she focused on the Fall 2015 cohort because it is the most recent cohort with available 2-year follow-up data to demonstrate how patterns endure over time. She used covariate adjustment to model how students were selected into DCMP and to examine the relationship between DCMP status and outcomes (e.g., persisting in college, passing developmental mathematics, enrolling in college mathematics, and passing college mathematics), while trying to control for the fact that DCMP students are quite different from those in a traditional mathematics pathway (Schudde and Keisler, 2019). In the Fall 2015 cohort (see Figure 3-7), students in DCMP were much more likely to be white than their counterparts in the traditional developmental mathematics pathway (44% versus 26%). There is a slightly higher representation of black students in DCMP than in traditional developmental education. However, Hispanic students were highly underrepresented in DCMP compared to traditional developmental education, which is of great concern given the high population overall of Hispanic students enrolled in Texas postsecondary institutions. DCMP students were also more likely to

Selection into DCMP (Fall 2015)

Student Background	DCMP	Other Dev-Ed
Race		
White	43.75%	25.71%***
Asian	1.14%	1.37%
Black	21.08%	16.16%***
Hispanic	31.27%	53.76%***
Other	2.76%	3.00%
Female	64.10%	60.79%***
Filed FAFSA	31.02%	29.75%†
Family Income (among FAFSA filers)	$47,753	$41,121**
N	4,461	24,394

Placement Test Measures	DCMP	Other Dev-Ed
Has TSI (placement test) score	67.88%	53.06%***
Average TSI (for students who had a score)	333.90	331.17***
Average z-score for any placement test	-0.56	-0.74***

†p>.1, *p>.05, **p>.01, ***p>.001

FIGURE 3-7 Profile of students served by the DCMP model versus the traditional developmental education sequence.
SOURCES: Schudde (2019, slides 11 and 12); data from Texas Higher Education Coordinating Board.

be women, to have higher income, and to have performed better on placement tests.

Schudde emphasized that these patterns of selection should be a cause for concern, especially because students who are enrolled in DCMP tend to have better outcomes than those in traditional pathways. DCMP students are more likely to enroll in college mathematics in the subsequent semester by 16 percentage points and are more likely to pass college mathematics by the end of that semester by 4 percentage points, and these patterns persisted over a 2-year span. Additionally, there is little evidence of differential effects, indicating that "everyone benefits," according to Schudde. These findings, she continued, align with those of the randomized control trial discussed by Zachry Rutschow (see Chapter 2) and hold true even at institutions that did not agree to a randomization study, suggesting that DCMP is working in a variety of contexts. But, essentially, "students who probably would have been more likely to get access to better opportunities anyway" are the ones who have the greatest access to DCMP, she explained. DCMP is intended for students who need acceleration (i.e., they placed two or three levels below college-level mathematics) and not necessarily intended for students who need only one semester. While the latter population of students might benefit from the curricular reform, they do not necessarily need the structural reform. Thus, Schudde commented that more research is needed, including a close examination of selection procedures to better understand the messages faculty and advisers are giving students about developmental mathematics and reform options, the role of implicit bias, and how students view mathematics placement in light of their beliefs about their mathematical abilities. Additionally, she emphasized the need to change current procedures and cultures that create inequitable opportunities for students: the goal is to ensure that students, advisers, and faculty are all informed about the negative effects of prolonged developmental education on student success and, as a result, to shift student course enrollment toward alternative pathways.

DISCUSSION

Building on Boatman's assertions about the outcomes for the Fall 2014 cohort of students, Denley commented that the structural changes via the co-requisite model had not been implemented at that time, and so more recent data indicate that both pedagogical and structural changes are needed to make the most beneficial gains for student success, especially for students at the low end of the preparation spectrum. Julie Phelps noted that Park-Gaghan's research motivated Florida postsecondary institutions to study their own data; mathematics faculty at Valencia College are now meeting once every other month to discuss these data, emerging questions, and possible reforms that better support students and close achievement gaps. Denley observed that front-line faculty in Georgia and Tennessee were initially unaware of the data they needed to enable reforms, and he reiterated Phelps's assertion that academic institutions need to have access to data about their own students. Melguizo emphasized the value of involving community college faculty in this work, which will inform practice, and engaging student voices in advocacy for reform.

Recalling her panel's discussion on equitable opportunities for students, Pamela Burdman asked these panelists if their research has illustrated anything about the theory behind versus the actual implementation of mathematics pathways. Schudde said that comparable numbers of students are actually pursuing the different pathway options and that instead of limiting students, mathematics pathways might be prompting them to enroll in more mathematics courses. Amy Getz, manager of systems implementation for higher education at the Charles A. Dana Center at The University of Texas at Austin, observed that Schudde's data provide evidence for supporting a 1-semester model instead of a 1-year model and for implementing reforms at full scale.

Denley cautioned reform advocates about stressing the "accelerated" nature of reform efforts, such as the co-requisite model, as that language can increase both student and faculty skepticism about their success; in reality, the co-requisite model is successful because parallel remediation is more effective than serial remediation. Hetts agreed that labeling courses (e.g., as "stretch" or "accelerated") could be dangerous because it signals incorrectly to students that one course could be easier than the other.

Zachry Rutschow referenced a soon-to-be-released randomized control trial study that she led on the mathematics pathways model. Noting that it was difficult to identify institutions willing to implement this curriculum at a high level, she confirmed how challenging it is to change instructor practice. Furthermore, a survey of a randomized group of students revealed that the mathematics pathways approach led to a 40 to 50 percent increase in students' positive experiences of how they learned mathematics, in their comprehension of how mathematics applies to their life experiences, and in their work with other students in small groups, as well as a decrease in the amount of traditional classroom lecture that they received. Schudde hypothesized that even more substantial positive effects might be observed if it were possible to control for students enrolled in other developmental mathematics education reforms (e.g., co-requisite model) in the research. Boatman shared similar findings from qualitative observations of the high school students in the Tennessee SAILS program: they felt better prepared for college upon completion of the program, and they better understood the usefulness of mathematics compared to students not enrolled in the program.

Treisman observed that when faculty recognize that students can succeed in college-level mathematics courses without taking prerequisite courses (i.e., developmental mathematics education courses), the powerful reality of "intelligent co-requisite design" becomes attainable. He pointed out that while faculty are essential components of pedagogical reform, structural reforms at scale are what lead to the dramatic increases in student success rates. Hetts shared a slightly different perspective in that faculty professional development opportunities have opened faculty members' minds to greater change, thus enabling structural reform at many institutions. Echoing Denley's earlier comment, Mesa emphasized that individual faculty cannot change the landscape of developmental mathematics education on their own; instructional reform must be paired with structural reform in order to enhance success for students. She explained that faculty professional development should be combined with a "structural understanding of how the system works, how we bias students into courses, how we do not listen in advising, and how we do not understand the needs that people have" in order to make full-scale improvements in mathematics education.

REFLECTIONS FROM DAY 1 OF THE WORKSHOP

After a series of thought-provoking presentations and panel discussions throughout the first day of the workshop, Phelps asked participants to reflect on these conversations and to share their perspectives about the current and future states of developmental mathematics education. Zachry Rutschow expressed her disappointment that despite the data that exist on reform, many 2-year institutions are still implementing mathematics reforms alongside traditional prerequisite sequences; thus, much work remains to be done to scale these reforms. Denley added that students do not need to be "fixed;" instead, structure, policy, and pedagogy need to be reformed to improve students' experiences, especially given that new approaches to delivering mathematics content seem to eliminate equity gaps. Treisman called for research specifically focused on the one-third of students who are still not being well served by mathematics reforms. Mark Green echoed Treisman's suggestion to consider why those students are not being well served and added that for the two-thirds of students who are already succeeding, additional support could be implemented to help them graduate and start successful careers. Zachry Rutschow agreed that instead of focusing only on methods to get students *through* college mathematics, educators should focus on how to get students *interested* in mathematics courses and careers. Thus, research is needed on how instructional reforms could change students' experiences with mathematics in these ways.

Phelps argued that connection and direction for students are imperative for student success, and faculty can learn lessons both from their colleagues and from data about how to impact futures by creating equitable outcomes for all students. Boatman added that academic institutions need guidance to understand how the data illuminate issues on their individual campuses, and Phelps urged workshop participants to replace the phrase "faculty buy-in" with "faculty engagement and ownership" when talking about faculty involvement with reform initiatives. Denley shared that a faculty community of instructional practice around reform initiatives is one approach that could help change this mentality about reform. As is the case in Georgia, by participating in these learning communities, faculty begin to share their experiences around implementation, change their mindsets, and own these structural changes, Denley explained.

Mesa pointed out that true reform takes time and involves politicians, legislators, and faculty alike. In the meantime, educators have the power to influence students' experiences in positive ways, Adiredja proposed. Schweingruber raised the issue of systemic reform, emphasizing that more research is needed to understand how to bring these reforms to scale (i.e., who the actors are and how to motivate policy change), and Treisman observed that periods of change offer opportunities to create new norms for responsible practice. For example, because eliminating barriers is not the same as achieving ultimate outcomes (e.g., earning high-value degrees in nursing, business accounting, information technology, etc.), a higher class of equity problems should be targeted and subjected to critical research study.

Other areas for opportunity include increased partnerships and participation across the K–12 and higher-education spaces, according to Schweingruber. Hetts agreed and emphasized the need to recognize K–12 colleagues for the high-quality instruction that they provide to students. Rebecca Fitch added that postsecondary institutions need to place more confidence in the K–12 system and its assessments of students (i.e., high school transcripts) instead of relying on standardized test scores for placement in college or developmental courses, since research has proven that those measures are ineffective and often lead to negative consequences.

To conclude the first day of the workshop, Amy Kerwin provided her reflections. She explained that Ascendium Education Group, the sponsor of the workshop, concentrates on learners from populations that are historically underrepresented in both postsecondary education and workforce training, especially those from low-income backgrounds. She thanked the Board on Science Education, the planning committee members, and the workshop speakers for their work to organize the workshop and to help create a set of important research questions to move reform efforts in the field forward. She reiterated the need to focus further research and reform initiatives on the three cohorts of students who are not being well served in the era of developmental mathematics education reform: (1) the 30 to 40 percent of students who are still not succeeding in current developmental mathematics sequences, (2) the students who are "structurally prevented" from accessing a developmental education reform pathway (e.g., an institution does not offer enough sections of the reform or offers biased advising), and (3) the students who cannot access any reform (e.g., students enrolled in a community-based adult basic education program). Kerwin championed the notion of implementing reforms "with a sense of fidelity to the spirit of the reform and not simply to the structure of the reform," but she cautioned that biases maintained by students, faculty, and advisers alike can interfere with achieving this vision. She emphasized that the mathematics education community has an opportunity to create a research agenda that "sends a clear signal to policy makers, to college and university leaders, to faculty, and ultimately to others in philanthropy that we really and truly do believe that math is for everyone." She lauded the many ideas about future areas of research that emerged from the panel discussions and presentations and shared her commitment to thinking collaboratively about the next steps following the workshop.

4

Promising Approaches for Transforming Developmental Mathematics Education

Opening the second day of the workshop, Susan Bickerstaff provided an overview of the topics and themes explored on the first day of the workshop. Workshop participants were introduced to a variety of reform strategies that are being implemented across the United States to improve student outcomes in mathematics (see Chapter 2), and they were presented with the evidence base to justify the adoption of these strategies (see Chapter 3). She observed that two central themes surfaced during these discussions: (1) the importance of faculty understanding the desired outcomes of their work, which include ensuring that students learn quantitative skills to be successful in their programs and careers, helping students develop their mathematical identities and find the joy in mathematics, providing students with viable pathways to careers of interest, and raising students' expectations of themselves and their capacities; and (2) classroom-level instruction is a promising area for future research, given the significant gains in student success that have been made with little to no large-scale change at the classroom level and the substantial portion of students who are not successful even in these new reform contexts.

The first day of the workshop also included interactive breaks, which afforded time and space for participants to discuss approaches to reforming developmental mathematics that had not yet been highlighted in the workshop and to identify approaches that, in their opinion, the field should try in order to increase student success in developmental mathematics. Bickerstaff shared excerpts from various whiteboard posts that emerged during these informal conversations. One participant reiterated that "negative math experiences leave an emotional trauma on the student," while another participant urged that students should be thought of as "producers of information" instead of "consumers of information." A third participant suggested that because "cultural capital is important in native communities for success in school, language and culture should be integrated with the curriculum as much as possible." Regarding students who might not yet be achieving success, another workshop participant referenced programs at Wright State University and at Indian River College that contextualize mathematics instruction in terms of individual disciplines. Similarly, another participant suggested that students should "learn the math after understanding the reason or importance to achieve their goal." Lastly, a participant expressed the need for the mathematics education community to "understand the impact of real-life issues for many developmental education students by combining efforts like single-stop or other holistic approaches with developmental mathematics reform to address the students who are still not succeeding." Reflecting on these contributions, Bickerstaff indicated how much time and how many resources are needed to implement these approaches—to curate and cultivate high-quality instructional materials, for faculty to have the reflective space and support to change their interactions with students, and to increase knowledge for the high proportion of part-time faculty of the college curriculum, student supports on campus, and the campus resources to support faculty.

Moving into the first panel of the second day of the workshop, Bickerstaff posed the following questions to serve as a guide for workshop participants:

- How do we increase access to approaches that we know improve student outcomes?
- How do we build on successes to meet the needs of students who continue to be left behind?

She expressed hoped that, during the remaining sessions of the workshop, participants would consider how to "center the student experience in mathematics." She suggested that the next phase of research should continue to identify limitations in the system, including the student groups that are not being well served; build faculty capacity for meeting students' needs; help understand something new about students' experiences, especially how they are learning; and illuminate key features of high-quality implementation of the most promising reforms, which is discussed in the following section.

A DEEPER LOOK AT FOUR
PROMISING MODELS FOR CHANGE

Tristan Denley noted that this session of the workshop would emphasize strategies to put the theory of reform into action. He moderated a panel discussion that explored four specific models of transformation in developmental mathematics education: (1) the University System of Georgia's adoption of the co-requisite model, (2) The University of Texas at Austin's creation of the Dana Center Mathematics Pathways, (3) the City University of New York's (CUNY's) conception of its innovative CUNY Start program, and (4) Carnegie's development of the Statway and Quantway mathematics pathways. These new models include changes in course structure, in curricular structure, in how faculty and administrators help students navigate the college experience, and in pedagogy, respectively. Denley presented four objectives for this panel discussion: (1) identify what is known about these strategies, (2) share challenges in bringing these programs to scale, (3) describe the potential of scaling these programs even further, and (4) define what is known about students who are and are not being well served by these new models.[1]

The Co-requisite Model

Denley explained that developmental education reform should enable students to be more successful in mathematics and to more successfully complete college. In a study of all University System of Georgia students, he found that students who passed their first credit-bearing mathematics and English courses during their first year of college had 6-year graduation rates twice that of their peers who passed only one or the other in the first year and 10 times that of their peers who completed neither course successfully in the first year.

In 2015, the University System of Georgia offered three approaches to developmental mathematics education: (1) the traditional developmental mathematics sequence; (2) the foundations model, in which students had to complete a semester-long remediation course successfully before enrolling in a college-level course; and (3) the co-requisite model, in which students enroll directly in a credit-bearing college mathematics course in their first year while also being required to enroll in an aligned supplementary instruction course.

Denley said that traditional structures of developmental mathematics create a barrier to student success. When the co-requisite model was fully

---

[1] Background resources on these models can be found at https://sites.nationalacademies.org/DBASSE/BOSE/devmathhandouts/index.htm.

implemented across community colleges in Tennessee in 2015–2016, 55 percent of students successfully completed a credit-bearing mathematics course in the first year. Previously, when students were placed in developmental mathematics first before being able to complete a college-level mathematics course, the success rate in the credit-bearing course was only 12.3 percent. Thus, in the year that the co-requisite model went to scale, more students passed a college-level mathematics class in Tennessee community colleges than in the previous 3 years combined. The University System of Georgia has been experiencing similar gains across the preparation spectrum with its implementation of the co-requisite model. Figure 4-1 shows that from a sample size of nearly 30,000 students in the University System of Georgia, the success rates in credit-bearing mathematics courses increased substantially across the preparation spectrum. For example, for students with an ACT mathematics subscore of 14, the success rate increased from 9 percent in 2013 to 56 percent with the implementation of the co-requisite model in 2015–2017. For students with an ACT mathematics subscore of 18, the success rate increased from 30 to 63 percent.[2]

Denley explained that these gains also hold true across student subpopulations (e.g., for Pell Grant recipients and African American students), essentially eliminating equity gaps. This demonstrates that students tend to succeed when remediation is provided in a just-in-time, parallel fashion, instead of when it is front loaded as a prerequisite course, he continued. Regarding student success rates in concurrent reforms such as mathematics pathways, he noted that more students take and pass precalculus after the co-requisite college algebra class (19% and 66%, respectively) than in the foundational model (7% and 47%, respectively). Moreover, when considering the fact that some of the students within the foundations model population also had to get through another prerequisite course first, the exponential decay effect becomes evident as one moves toward the credit-bearing course level, similar to what Angela Boatman's work showed (see Chapter 3, Figure 3-4). Owing to the success of the co-requisite model and its ability to "unlock the promise" of many of the other kinds of reforms, all 26 campuses in the University System of Georgia offered only the co-requisite model for developmental mathematics (and English) education as of Fall 2018.

Dana Center Mathematics Pathways

Amy Getz stated that after listening to the discussions among participants throughout the first day of the workshop, she changed her

---

[2] According to Zachry Rutschow (2019), a score lower than 19 on the ACT generally indicates that a student is in need of additional skill development prior to being ready for college-level coursework.

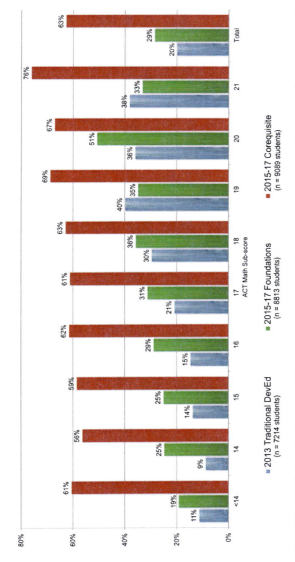

FIGURE 4-1 University System of Georgia comparison of success in gateway mathematics classes systemwide.
SOURCES: Denley (2019, slide 8), data from University System of Georgia.

presentation title to "Three reasons why this should be the last event that has the word 'developmental mathematics' in the title." She explained that the phrase "developmental mathematics" is problematic and should be eliminated from the lexicon of the mathematics education community. First, it implies that targeting and addressing only one small aspect of a student's education can alter the course of his/her future. Second, evidence has shown that traditional approaches to developmental mathematics are ineffective, especially given that both identifying and measuring college readiness is not well understood (Liston and Getz, 2019). Third, the concept of developmental mathematics creates more inequities in a system already filled with inequities. It is important to move to a scale of transformative education that benefits and provides "meaningful learning experiences" to all students, she explained.

Getz highlighted the benefits of the "mathematics pathways" perspective, which focuses on where students are coming from and where they would like to go. A pathways approach requires an understanding of students' strengths and previous experiences; faculty can then design intentional learning experiences to help students achieve their career goals (see Figure 4-2). The Dana Center Mathematics Pathways (DCMP) are based on four principles: (1) all students enter directly into mathematics pathways aligned to their programs of study; (2) courses are structured so that all students, regardless of college readiness, complete their first college-level mathematics requirement in the first year of college; (3) strategies to support students as learners should be integrated into courses and aligned across the institution; and (4) instruction should be based on evidence-based curriculum and pedagogy.[3] The first two principles are focused on structure, and the latter are centered on continuous improvement to ensure effective high-quality instruction. Additionally, Getz explained that these principles are "student-centered, faculty-led, administrator-supported, policy-enabled, and culturally reinforced."

Getz recognized that implementation will vary across institutions, so standards that guide the design of successful reform and empower local leaders to tailor approaches to the needs of their students would be beneficial. Both structural and policy changes are needed quickly and at scale (Charles A. Dana Center, 2018), she continued. Getz reiterated that to be equipped to adopt new approaches that better serve students, faculty and administrators have to be willing to continually learn from data, which ensures that ineffective practices do not become embedded in the system. For instance, the DCMP started out with a 1-year model, but after looking

---

[3] For more information about the DCMP principles, see https://dcmathpathways.org/dcmp/dcmp-model.

TRANSFORMING DEVELOPMENTAL MATHEMATICS EDUCATION

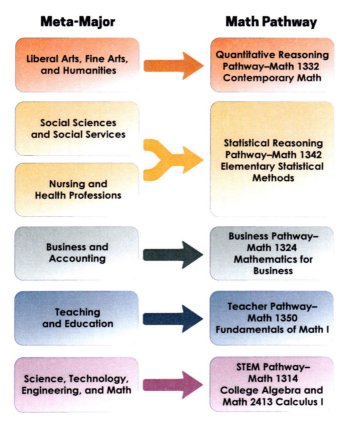

FIGURE 4-2 Example of aligning mathematics with the needs of students based on their majors.
SOURCES: Getz (2019, slide 4), data from Charles A. Dana Center.

at the data and determining that there was a better way to serve students, the approach was changed to a one-semester model.

CUNY Start

Jeanette Kim, interim university assistant dean for Pre-Matriculation Programs and Program Assessment at CUNY, described her institution as the largest urban university system in the United States, with 25 campuses and more than 240,000 undergraduates—97,000 of whom are seeking associate's degrees. She noted that more than 58 percent of CUNY's students are black or Hispanic, 40 percent have household incomes below $20,000, and 65 percent of first-time associate degree students have one or more remedial needs. Kim discussed several steps toward remediation reform that CUNY is taking, including the expansion of co-requisites and the elimination of traditional placement testing. Her presentation highlighted the CUNY Start program, which allows students to take advantage of the prematriculation space to address their remedial needs.

The CUNY Start program provides intensive preparation in reading, writing, mathematics, and college success to students who are admitted to CUNY but whose ACCUPLACER[4] test scores indicate significant need for remediation. These students defer matriculation for one semester while beginning the program for a low fee as either full-time students (25 hours per week for $75) or part-time students (12 hours per week for $35), over a semester, a summer, or a series of 8-week intensive sessions. One intensive adviser is assigned to every 25 students, with the goal of preparing them academically, socially, and emotionally for college. Faculty are trained via apprenticeship models, and the CUNY Start program is coordinated through a central office. CUNY Start has been implemented at seven community colleges and three senior colleges—the annual CUNY Start enrollment of approximately 4,300 students is 57 percent female, 78 percent black and Hispanic, and 75 percent under age 24. The CUNY Start mathematics program focuses specifically on developing students' growth mindsets, promoting conceptual understanding, and emphasizing collaborative learning. Upon completion of the program, students take the CUNY elementary algebra final exam, which is a systemwide exit standard for remediation; this consistent measure demonstrates that CUNY Start students are held to the same standards as other CUNY students, Kim explained.

Kim believes that CUNY Start has been successful because it eliminates or reduces students' remedial needs before they matriculate into their degree programs (see Figure 4-3), saves financial aid for credit-bearing coursework, demands intensive cohort-based learning, exposes students to highly trained faculty and advisers, and increases the likelihood that students will persist and graduate. She shared the findings of an ongoing MDRC study of the first 9 years of the CUNY Start program, which revealed that CUNY Start students made more progress through their remedial requirements than the control students, especially in mathematics (Scrivener et al., 2018). She also highlighted data from a quasi-experimental analysis that revealed that CUNY Start students were outperforming the matched comparison group in both credit-bearing English and mathematics courses, and this advantage was maintained after 2 years (see Jenkins Webber, 2018).

---

[4] ACCUPLACER diagnostic assessments identify the knowledge, strength, and needs of students in math, reading, and writing, for placement into classes that match students' skill levels. For more information on ACCUPLACER, see https://accuplacer.collegeboard.org.

TRANSFORMING DEVELOPMENTAL MATHEMATICS EDUCATION 63

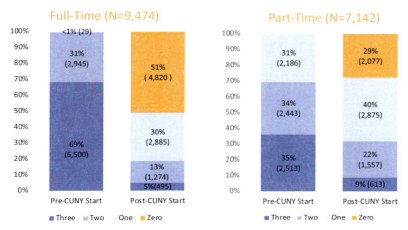

FIGURE 4-3 The number of developmental education needs is significantly reduced after completion of the CUNY Start program.
SOURCES: Kim (2019, slide 7), data from CUNY Start program database.

Kim mentioned that now that the program has proven successful for students with deep remedial needs, CUNY is working to identify other populations it is not yet serving. It is engaging with nontraditional students, including precollege populations, returning adult learners, and students who have achieved high school equivalency but have failed certain mathematics requirements. CUNY Start is also trying to identify students who have failed traditional developmental mathematics courses twice in order to provide these students with the needed supports to avoid being dismissed from the institution. Lastly, CUNY Start is creating a pipeline for students to move into CUNY Accelerated Study in Associate Programs (see Chapter 2 and Chapter 5) to continue to receive intensive wraparound support as they move toward college completion.

Carnegie Mathematics Pathways (Statway and Quantway)

Karon Klipple, executive director of the Carnegie Mathematics Pathways at WestEd, shared that of the 1.1 million first-time students enrolling in community college each year, 60 percent are placed in remedial mathematics courses, and only 20 percent will ever complete a single college-level mathematics course. In 2010, the Carnegie Foundation for the

> "Of the 1.1 million first-time students enrolling in community college each year, 60 percent are placed in remedial mathematics courses, and only 20 percent will ever complete a single college-level mathematics course."

Advancement of Teaching[5] convened researchers, practitioners, faculty, and students to consider this problem in developmental education and create a holistic solution. The solution addressed the structure of developmental mathematics education, challenged the notion of what mathematics content students need to learn and when they need to learn it, and engaged students in "relevant and meaningful" mathematics "in a way that supported active, collaborative learning where they could bring their own experiences to bear on solving a problem." She highlighted the many factors beyond mathematics content and instruction that can affect student success (e.g., a student's mindset about his/her mathematical abilities and a student's sense of belonging in both the mathematics classroom and on the college campus). With this in mind, she continued, comprehensive supports were needed to prepare faculty to teach in a new way, as well as collective action to ensure continuous improvement over time based on what the data revealed.

As a result of this effort, two mathematics pathways were created by the Carnegie Foundation for the Advancement of Teaching: Statway and Quantway. Approximately 100 institutions and 40,000 students have been involved in this reform. According to Klipple, the programs generate triple the success in half the time (see Figure 4-4) as traditional approaches to developmental education, with 70 percent of the pathways students earning college-level credits. These results hold across all racial, ethnic, and gender subgroups. Statway and Quantway students also succeed with higher grades in upper-division mathematics courses, which indicates that there is a deeper level of learning happening in the pathways programs, she continued. These students are also earning 4-year degrees at more than two times the rate of their matched peers.

Klipple emphasized that there are still approximately 500,000 students enrolled in traditional developmental mathematics sequences annually who

---

[5]The Carnegie Foundation for the Advancement of Teaching aims to build a field around the use of improvement science and networked improvement communities to solve longstanding inequities in educational outcomes. For more information, see https://www.carnegiefoundation.org.

TRANSFORMING DEVELOPMENTAL MATHEMATICS EDUCATION 65

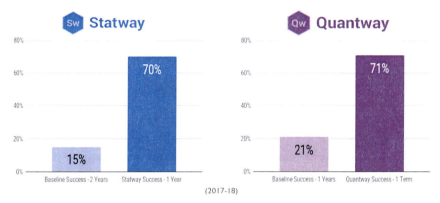

FIGURE 4-4 Success of Statway and Quantway students in 2017–2018 in earning college-level credits as compared to students who enroll in a traditional developmental mathematics sequence.
SOURCES: Klipple (2019, Slide 6), data from WestEd.

are unable to continue in college and achieve their career goals. She said that the mathematics education community has a moral imperative to reform developmental education and eliminate its barriers to success.

DISCUSSION

Presenters discussed the challenges that arise when taking these strategies to scale. One common experience across the models was that access to and an understanding of data were key in persuading institutions and faculty to implement mathematics education reforms. Getz noted that many states do not have ready access to data or a system to support cross-institutional action, and it is important to think about different ways to navigate those problems. Coordinating action across multiple institutions is challenging, but it is necessary to promote student success throughout their college careers, given that students often transfer into and out of institutions along the way, she continued. Denley emphasized that creating a data structure to prove that the co-requisite model was effective had been necessary to motivate both the Tennessee community colleges and the University System of Georgia to adopt the approach. An institution's ability to evaluate its own data, as opposed to looking at the data of students at other institutions, is necessary to design and execute programs in a way that will benefit an institution's unique students, he explained. However, even with data, faculty remained skeptical about how the co-requisite approach would work for a variety of populations of students until a prototype was created in Tennessee. This prototype allowed faculty to learn lessons quickly about a variety of issues (e.g., logistics, faculty recruitment, faculty training, etc.) in order to take the co-requisite model to scale.

Kim commented that in terms of scaling opportunities, the CUNY Start program's challenge stems from the fact that it is based on referrals and students opt into the program. New strategies are needed to identify and enroll more students who would benefit from the program, taking into consideration the substantial time commitment that is required of them. Klipple emphasized the value of having champions across an institution—faculty can change what happens in the classroom and administrators can facilitate policies for hiring, advising, transfer, placement, evaluation, and resource allocation. These initiatives cannot be successful when individuals are running pilot programs; the work has to be institutionalized with the support of a broad group of stakeholders who are motivated by the data and inspired to make change, she continued. Still, she explained, challenges remain in understanding how to measure the success of reform efforts accurately, given the heterogeneity of the students being served, and how to help students who are still not succeeding even within these new contexts. Klipple asserted that some of these students might not be succeeding owing to a lack of support for the social-emotional component of learning. Denley agreed and noted that some students might not have developed a sense of social belonging and inclusion in their mathematics courses. Additionally, he shared that work is under way in Georgia to better understand the effects of academic mindset interventions, including social belonging strategies. Philip Uri Treisman suggested that workshop participants review the work of Catherine Good, of Baruch College, to better understand how the absence of a sense of belonging can negatively impact student success in science, technology, engineering, and mathematics pathways.

Several participants highlighted that discussions about student success in the era of reform often include concerns about academic rigor. Ann Sitomer, senior researcher at Oregon State University, said that she found it "difficult to believe that any co-requisite model leads to the outcomes presented by Denley." She asked, "What are the mathematical features that lead to these outcomes?" Denley noted that the mathematics course in the co-requisite model is identical to the traditional credit-bearing course, and Klipple affirmed that these new mathematics education models have the same level of rigor and expectations for students as traditional credit-bearing courses. If the rigor is the same, Maxine Roberts wondered, what is it about the supports that are making such a difference in student success? Klipple emphasized that students are more accurately placed into these courses and are provided with the support they need to be successful in college-level mathematics. Furthermore, the problems they are learning to solve do not rely on disconnected, irrelevant mathematical concepts. The cohort structure is also particularly valuable in that it allows faculty to assess and target students' needs individually and offer the right supports, she continued. Denley asserted that having just-in-time remediation is more effective for students, and the co-requisite model eliminates the fundamental "othering" of being a developmental mathematics student, which can derail student success. Getz added that just-in-time remediation also better aligns course content.

Given Klipple's revelation that 500,000 students are still not benefitting from reform efforts, Mark Green asked how members of academia, the National Academies, and professional societies could help to scale these efforts appropriately. Getz asserted, "We have to make it really clear that it is not acceptable to ignore data anymore; that is just professional malpractice." She emphasized that professional societies have a strong role in setting standards about what it means to be a mathematics educator and in changing faculty mindsets. Treisman observed that some campuses are inappropriately applying reform language to describe traditional approaches, and he urged the mathematics education community to "mount a massive effort to set standards of responsible practice" to combat these inadequate strategies. Denley described an "astonishing change" in the messages around the different nonalgebra mathematics pathways following the work of Transforming Post-Secondary Education in Mathematics (TPSE), which has begun to work with the mathematics education community to develop content that is pertinent to students' disciplines. Because TPSE, he continued, has endorsed the statistics and quantitative reasoning mathematics pathways, many of the narratives suggesting that these pathways are not synonymous with rigor have changed immeasurably. Denley also called on the mathematics community to similarly affirm the co-requisite model as the best way forward in mathematics education and the English community to undertake similar work. Julie Phelps added that the majority of submissions to the 2019 American Mathematical Association of Two-Year Colleges Conference highlighted reformed approaches instead of traditional developmental mathematics—of the 300 proposals received, approximately 20 retained the traditional phrases "developmental education" or "remedial math." Another indication that transformation is under way throughout the professional societies is the decision of the National Association for Developmental Education to change its name to the National Organization for Student Success, she continued.

SYNERGY OF MATHEMATICS REFORM EFFORTS AND OVERALL STRATEGIES TO TRANSFORM UNDERGRADUATE EDUCATION

As the discussion of scaling promising models for change continues, it is important to consider the larger-scale changes that are occurring within and across undergraduate programs in U.S. postsecondary institutions, said Treisman. Serving as the moderator of the panel that discussed the synergy of mathematics reform efforts and overall strategies to transform undergraduate education, Treisman went on to say that the failure of developmental education is *not* a result of any failings on the part of people who have devoted their lives to supporting students. Instead, he described developmental education as a failed policy response to fundamental changes in higher education in the 1950s and 1960s, to the GI Bill, and to the civil rights movement, all of which dramatically increased enrollment in higher education. Additionally, he continued, the launch of the Soviet Union's Sputnik 1 in the 1950s and international competitiveness put pressure on U.S. mathematics departments to produce high-end scientists.

Treisman explained that in his perspective reforms, to developmental mathematics education gained traction with the recession of 2008, when financial challenges and enrollment crises in the United States motivated institutions to focus on improving student success. At the same time, professional organizations began to change their standards of responsible practice, issuing strong policy statements that reinforced the mathematics pathways movement. He emphasized that reforms in mathematics education do not stand alone; they are happening in the context of fundamental changes in approaches to advising, student orientation, and financial aid. Therefore, he continued, there must be "mutually reinforcing synergy" with overall strategies to transform undergraduate education.

Treisman was joined on the panel by Nyema Mitchell, a senior program manager at Jobs for the Future, and Rahim Rajan, deputy director of the Postsecondary Division at the Bill & Melinda Gates Foundation. Mitchell's work supports 16 Student Success Centers[6] located across the country, which are scaling guided pathways programs in their respective states in the context of unique policy environments. Rajan works on a team that is concentrating on evidence-based interventions, practices, tools, and technologies to enhance student success and to erase equity gaps for students of color, low-income students, and adult learners.

Rajan explained that, in the past 10 years, the emphasis in higher education has shifted from access to success. Now, another shift is occurring toward understanding the markers of success, and now a holistic, comprehensive set of reforms and transformational strategies (e.g., in capacities, processes, and structures) need to be implemented to best serve students, he continued. The mathematics reforms discussed in the context of this workshop "are a part of a suite of efforts that fundamentally change the

---

[6]For more information about these Student Success Centers, see https://www.jff.org/what-we-do/impact-stories/student-success-center-network.

normative practice on a campus," but, Rajan continued, these efforts are insufficient. He asserted that this work is "fundamentally about improving the lives of Americans and overcoming poverty. And higher education is still that lever to do that, but it requires broad change and reform in order to really tap that potential for individuals."

Treisman asked the panelists how their organizations' supports have changed to reflect the shift from programmatic to systemic reforms as well as where more support is needed. Mitchell said that cross-sector partnerships are essential for understanding what kinds of change are supported by policy in each state. Thus, Jobs for the Future, she continued, has evolved to better assist the Student Success Centers in making data-informed decisions and positioning themselves to take advantage of the opportunities to institute reforms that will be taken up in their respective states. Rajan pointed to the Gates Foundation as an organization that takes a systems approach to address the kind of supports still needed in the field, and so co-invested in building a national network (e.g., Strong Start to Finish) that is focused on helping systems to scale their reforms. Acknowledging the efforts required to scale reforms, he added that no single funding entity can address this issue alone. Treisman asked the panelists to draw on their own experiences in helping to bring reforms to scale and to comment on the financial viability of these new models. Rajan expressed his disappointment that although it is more expensive for an institution to recruit new students than it is to help existing students succeed, reforms are still not being implemented at scale. This evidence justifies the need for institutions to invest in reform supports, such as integrated advising or social-emotional support, which will aid in student success, he continued.

Observing that systemic reforms depend on transfer and applicability policies, Treisman noted that a governance problem exists: institutions serving the same community of students (e.g., a high school and a community college located in the same town) lack a governing arrangement to allow for shared responsibility of this population. As a starting point to address this issue, Mitchell proposed the creation of additional infrastructure that states could use to exchange lessons learned while trying to overcome specific barriers during reform implementation. Following up on that concept, Treisman asked if there are emerging issues for undergraduate institutions more broadly, and Mitchell replied that offering courses that transfer from 2- to 4-year institutions remains a key barrier in helping students transition between campuses. Noting that 40 percent of community colleges in the state of Texas have high school students comprising 25 percent of their enrollment, Treisman reiterated that the boundaries between K–12 and higher education are fundamentally changing; he wondered about the leading edge of innovation to manage this transition and to align pathways. Rajan pointed to the University of Central Florida, which has partnerships with the local community colleges, like Valencia College, and the Orange County Public School system, as an example of the deep integration that is necessary to structure and align pathways across systems. With this infrastructure, all parties are involved in the co-development of the pathways requirements. Students who graduate from an Orange County public high school can automatically enroll at Valencia College, and Valencia College graduates have automatic acceptance to the University of Central Florida. Mitchell added that lessons learned in Florida could be applicable in a number of other states but that broad-scale reform requires consideration of local and state-level politics.

When panelists invited workshop participants to share their commentary on the synergy between reforms in mathematics education and those in undergraduate education more broadly, Ted Coe, director of mathematics at Achieve, suggested that conversations about college readiness should align with discussions about career readiness (e.g., determining what mathematics courses might be needed by students in an associate's program for future careers and spreading that message). Treisman agreed, noting that future careers could involve the sophisticated management of information (i.e., mathematical decision making) and the integration of computation (e.g., computing, statistical ideas, and mathematical analysis from algebra, calculus, etc.). For those who might cross industry sectors, Treisman continued, generalized problem solving will become increasingly important, as will the ability to develop quantitative competence through continued learning. Tatiana Melguizo said that it is essential to think about establishing "regions or corridors of success" (i.e., introducing the idea of guided pathways across sectors beginning with a large high school district, then moving to community colleges, and finally to 4-year institutions) when thinking about systemic reform. This approach would increase cross-sector collaboration to design courses, which might in turn decrease trust issues among faculty. Rajan added that when connecting these sectors, it is crucial not to overlook the students, especially students of color or low-income students who might have only one chance at higher education. Emphasizing that sometimes the best efforts can have adverse equity effects when changes are not implemented at scale, Treisman suggested building a pathway for students from the junior year of high school to the junior year of college that reflects the best mathematics (e.g., integrated use of computing, analysis, and statistics) that is oriented and organized around the future work that they will do in their careers. This would ensure that students have opportunities to be exposed early to coursework in emerging fields, such as big data, which might not be offered at all community colleges, he continued.

In closing the panel discussion, Rajan asked workshop participants how philanthropic organizations could be supportive of the remaining work needed to transform developmental mathematics education. Cammie Newmyer urged philanthropists to direct their attention toward rural areas and other pockets of high poverty. Getz commented that philanthropic organizations could help institutions access data and develop resources to track data over time. John Hetts added that support is needed to conduct more qualitative research, alongside the quantitative work, to evaluate the fidelity of reform implementations. Vilma Mesa requested that philanthropists lobby for increased education appropriations from the states to implement reforms at scale. Denley agreed that investments are needed to change the paradigm of developmental mathematics education. April Strom, professor of mathematics at Chandler–Gilbert Community College and a vice president of the American Mathematical Association of Two-Year Colleges, suggested funding for community college faculty to engage in partnerships with K–12 faculty and to support the development of K–16 professional development centers. Phelps agreed that community college faculty should be supported to engage in these conversations and to help design reform implementation strategies. Linda Braddy asked philanthropists to help raise awareness, especially among faculty and administrators, about the equity agenda. Treisman concluded by saying that the current role of philanthropy is to think about the "innovation that is needed at the current and next stages of this reform and how philanthropy can finish a set of initiatives that it [already] initiated, rather than just starting [new ones]."

5

Building Capacity to Meet the Needs of Students

During the previous session of the workshop, Rahim Rajan described the importance of focusing on students' needs when scaling developmental mathematics education reforms. Vilma Mesa moderated a panel on the second day of the workshop about how to build capacity within institutions to meet students' needs in this era of reform. Panelist April Strom, professor of mathematics at Chandler–Gilbert Community College and a vice president of the American Mathematical Association of Two-Year Colleges (AMATYC), contributed to the classroom practices chapter of the *Mathematical Association of America (MAA) Instructional Practices Guide* (Mathematical Association of America, 2018) and served on the Steering Committee for AMATYC's instructional standards guide, *IMPACT: Improving Mathematical Prowess and College Teaching* (American Mathematical Association of Two-Year Colleges, 2018). Panelist Karon Klipple, executive director of the Carnegie Mathematics Pathways at WestEd, leads the Network Improvement Community, which includes more than 100 U.S. postsecondary institutions working together to "change how students learn mathematics and gain the skills they need to be successful in their careers and their lives." Panelist Christine Brongniart is the interim university executive director of the City University of New York's (CUNY's) Accelerated Study in Associate Programs (ASAP), where she supports a nationally recognized associate degree completion program that has since been replicated in four states. Mesa shared that the objective of this panel is to share insights on the implementation of high-quality instruction, the development of resources and best practices for faculty, and the creation of relevant wraparound supports all in the service of effectively supporting students in introductory and developmental mathematics courses.

REFORMING INSTRUCTIONAL PRACTICES

Strom began her presentation by discussing high-quality instruction as a key part of achieving student success in mathematics classrooms. High-quality instruction builds students' conceptual knowledge through active learning, contextualized problem solving, and student-led solution methods (Zachry Rutschow, 2019). Strom mentioned that several professional societies have established task forces and published documents to help faculty think about why and how to implement high-quality instruction in their classrooms. She provided an overview of one of these efforts, the MAA's Common Vision Project, which identified common curricular themes in the documents of five mathematics and statistics organizations (see Figure 5-1).

Strom explained that two themes that are especially important for the instructional reform needed in developmental mathematics education are that the status quo is unacceptable and that active learning methods should replace more traditional lecturing approaches in the classroom. The *MAA Instructional Practices Guide* emerged from the Common Vision Project as a tool for faculty to use to implement high-quality instruction, and it has been used most recently to train graduate teaching assistants. This guide, and the chapter on classroom practices in particular, suggests that fostering student engagement and sense of belonging begins by building community

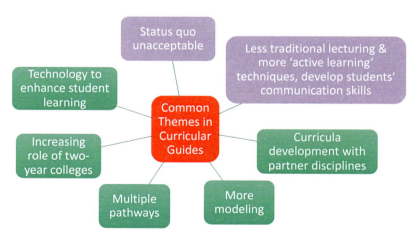

FIGURE 5-1 Seven common themes found across the curricular guides from mathematics professional societies as part of the MAA Common Vision Project.
SOURCE: Strom (2019, slide 2).

within a classroom—connecting students to one another, to the instructor, and to the discipline of mathematics (Mathematical Association of America, 2018).

Strom noted that AMATYC also produced an influential document on high-quality instruction: *Improving Mathematical Prowess and College Teaching* (IMPACT), a faculty-led effort to revise standards for teaching, learning, assessment, evaluation, and professional development in the mathematics offered in the first 2 years of college. This guide offers strategies to expand students' mathematical proficiency, to help students develop "ownership" of mathematics learning, to foster intellectual curiosity and motivation in the learning of mathematics (for both students and instructors), and to stimulate student achievement in mathematics (American Mathematical Association of Two-Year Colleges, 2018).

THE ROLE OF FACULTY IN ENHANCING STUDENT LEARNING

Klipple shared her perspectives on the important role that faculty play in helping to meet the diverse needs of developmental mathematics students at the level of instruction, and described specific ways in which faculty need to be prepared to facilitate new modes of learning and engagement in the classroom. She introduced the notions of routine and flexible expertise (see Hatano and Inagaki, 1986). Routine expertise is the ability to know how to use a procedure to solve a problem. However, she continued, routine expertise is difficult to apply to new challenges or in new contexts, and so it is essential that faculty also help students to develop flexible expertise, which requires critical thinking and conceptual understanding. Helping students to develop both routine and flexible expertise will allow them to understand why procedures work as well as to apply and extend procedures to new situations. She explained that faculty need to create an environment in which students are involved in three recurring and sustained learning opportunities in order for them to gain flexible expertise:

1. Students should interact and grapple with rich mathematics content (i.e., "productive struggle") to which they have to bring their own knowledge and experiences to bear, in order to expand their knowledge-base and problem-solving techniques.
2. Students should develop the ability to "make explicit connections between concepts and procedures" both within and across courses and disciplines.
3. Students should engage in "deliberate practice" that becomes both more challenging and more diverse over time.

Klipple shared that faculty need particular supports in order to create classrooms that offer these opportunities, and effective professional development to prepare them in this way should have the following characteristics:

- Flexible and responsive to faculty needs—emphasizing real-world problems and contexts that faculty encounter on their campuses.
- Designed for collaboration and social learning—affording opportunities for faculty to learn through active engagement.
- Grounded in real teaching—providing space for faculty to observe high-quality teaching in action.
- Job-embedded—creating opportunities for faculty to experiment with new approaches in their classrooms.
- Sustained over an extended period of time—offering training opportunities on a regular basis.

The Carnegie Math Pathways Faculty Support Program, in particular, offers various forms of engagement for faculty, including workshops, virtual training, and peer mentorship.

IMPLEMENTING WRAPAROUND SUPPORT FOR STUDENTS

A third approach highlighted to meet the needs of students is wraparound support, and Brongniart shared about the experiences of students who receive additional supports both within and outside of the classroom through CUNY ASAP.[1] She described CUNY ASAP as a "common sense approach to comprehensive wraparound support for students," and provided an overview of the program's components, including the following:

- *Structured pathways*—Consolidated full-time course schedules, first-year blocked courses, and winter and summer courses.
- *Comprehensive supports*—High-touch, individualized advisement; career readiness development; academic support services; and early engagement.
- *Financial resources*—Tuition gap waivers, textbook stipend, and transportation support.

CUNY ASAP serves 25,000 students across nine institutions in the CUNY system and is run through the Office of Academic Affairs. By using data intentionally and embracing faculty feedback, CUNY can provide

---

[1] CUNY ASAP is an appropriate next step toward college completion for many students who were enrolled in the CUNY Start program discussed in Chapter 4.

structured and clear pathways to graduation for students. Students are successful in CUNY ASAP owing to early engagement and connectivity afforded by the cohort model, she explained. The model has been replicated at three community colleges in the state of Ohio, with the support of Ascendium Education Group, and new plans include implementing the program in the San Mateo County Community College District in California. Additionally, the program has been adapted for two of CUNY's senior colleges—John Jay College of Criminal Justice and Lehman College—as the Accelerate, Complete, and Engage[2] [ACE] Program, providing 4 years of support[3] in an effort to double the 4-year graduation rate.

Brongniart said that CUNY ASAP has had a doubling effect on 3-year graduation rates over the past 12 years (see Figure 5-2 for a representation of this trend in the Fall 2007 through Fall 2014 cohorts), and early analysis of the replicated program in Ohio indicates similar success. By welcoming all eligible full-time, first-time freshmen into the program at Bronx Community College, it will be possible to better understand the implications of wraparound supports on systemic reform. She added that with the program expanding at this scale, increased investment in technology and tools to support advising will be needed.

DISCUSSION

Observing that it can be difficult for faculty to change their instructional practices, Mesa wondered how to embed high-quality instruction in all developmental courses and how to use institutional resources to support faculty in "this era of math pathways." Quoting her mentor Pat Thompson, Strom noted that "changing one's teaching practices is as hard as changing somebody's personality." She emphasized that investing in professional development that engages faculty in activities that they would actually do with their students is the first step to implementing high-quality instruction. She described active learning classrooms as a "game changer," in which faculty provide the mechanisms to encourage students to *think*. Access to high-quality materials is essential, and faculty need to be engaged in sustained, coherent, and meaningful professional development, Strom continued. She added that faculty would benefit from 100 hours of professional development each year. Klipple agreed with Strom that institutions should commit to faculty development and align their resources accordingly. She asserted that it is imperative to make space and time for faculty to improve their practice, and that one way to achieve this is to engage faculty as stakeholders in the process, making data about students visible to them to

---

[2] For more information about the ACE program, see https://www.jjay.cuny.edu/ace-john-jay.
[3] This model provides 2 years of support to transfer students.

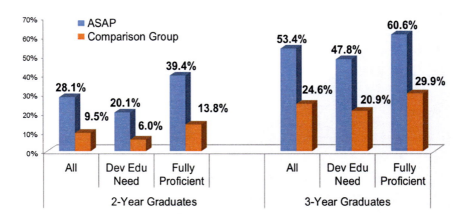

FIGURE 5-2 Two-year and 3-year graduation rates of students who received wraparound supports through CUNY ASAP (blue color) compared to control group (orange color) from Fall 2007 through Fall 2014.
SOURCES: Brongniart (2019, slide 5), data from City University of New York Institutional Research Database.

motivate change. Implementation of high-quality instructional practices, she continued, requires a cultural change for faculty, and although that could be difficult, many faculty are eager for opportunities to re-envision their roles, and these cultural changes could eventually transform faculty hiring and evaluation processes.

Mesa wondered about the cost to implement such extensive programs and suggested performing an analysis to understand how much these initiatives would save an academic institution over time if students persisted as a result. Klipple referenced prior work on the return on investment for pathways that engaged faculty in this kind of professional development. In the course of evaluating more than six institutions, it became clear that the return on investment was positive for all of these institutions and more than 50 percent for many of them. Brongniart said that CUNY has performed an extensive cost/benefit analysis of its support programs. Although up-front costs to support faculty and students are significant, especially to maintain dedicated personnel and to replicate the program, the returns to the taxpayer and to the institution are apparent. Klipple reiterated Rajan's previous point that although it is more expensive for an institution to recruit new students than it is to help existing students succeed, reforms are still not being implemented at scale. She emphasized that a failure to invest now will negatively impact students, especially their economic mobility.

With consideration for such expansive changes, Mesa inquired about other types of resources that might be needed over the long term to best serve the populations of students who are not prepared for college. Brongniart pointed to CUNY ASAP as an example, remarking that the program is built on a public-sector partnership (curated through support of the city of New York) that relies on data on best practices to "serve students and propel their academic momentum." By tracking students' academic and engagement data, both individually and in the aggregate, program leaders can better understand how students' progress through a holistic model such as CUNY ASAP and, more specifically, how students are impacted by it. In addition to the resources enabled by this partnership, CUNY ASAP relies on the support of academic advisors to be "navigators" for students while they acclimate and learn to make decisions about their academic futures.

Mesa asked the panelists to consider how to overcome any other significant challenges for successful implementation of these initiatives at scale. Strom explained that although national-level data are useful, local-level data are crucial. She emphasized the value of qualitative research from community college instructors to better understand what is and is not enhancing mathematics learning in the classroom. She and Mesa are engaged in such a study with support from the National Science Foundation, for which they are watching 400 hours of videotaped instruction from 88 community college instructors. She encouraged others to participate in similar research. Klipple reiterated that champions are needed to initiate change, and leaders are needed to institutionalize change. No longer can initiatives afford to operate as pilots; prototype-to-scale is the ideal model, she continued. Brongniart agreed and reaffirmed that ASAP's goal is to *not* be relevant anymore—when reforms occur at full scale, common sense practices are applied across the spectrum to meet the needs of all students: full-time, part-time, and transfer populations.

The panelists invited workshop participants to share their perspectives on building capacity within institutions to better meet the needs of students. Aditya Adiredja reiterated his suggestion from the first day of the workshop to infuse issues such as racism, sexism, and ableism into this discussion and into the research about how faculty can better serve students. Strom agreed that educators should better understand how to identify equity issues and how to overcome them, both in reforming teaching practices and in implementing appropriate course content. The mathematics education community, she continued, could spark these conversations locally, especially for faculty who do not have the resources to attend national workshops and conferences. Mesa urged that students, especially underrepresented students in science, technology, engineering, and mathematics, be reminded that they deserve to be in college-level courses and that they are capable of succeeding. She suggested that professional development that imbues issues about historical oppression is necessary for faculty to become more sensitive to the challenges that some of their students face.

Referring back to Brongniart's remarks about intensive advising as a mechanism for student success, Heidi Schweingruber wondered about building capacity, in terms of professional development for advisers to do intensive advising, which would potentially be very different from what some of them may be used to. In response, Brongniart explained that dedicated training in intensive advising helps academic advisers to become comfortable with identifying students' individual needs and then tailoring the modality and frequency of interaction with those students appropriately. Because advising relationships tend to be established around "academic progress momentum," which can be interpreted in various ways, Brongniart said that it is important to build a foundation and develop shared competencies between faculty and academic advisers. Philip Uri Treisman noted that innovative, time-consuming teaching experiences tend only to attract 10–15 percent of faculty, so he wondered how to engage more faculty in structural reform initiatives. Klipple acknowledged this problem but noted that she has encountered institutions where at least half of the faculty are involved in these labor-intensive initiatives. Strom suggested that the expectations and incentives for educators be increased; educators should think of themselves as lifelong learners who continually take advantage of opportunities to do their jobs better. Schweingruber added that different models of professional development be considered for 2- and 4-year institution faculty, as these two populations have unique issues.

Given the differential outcomes for CUNY ASAP students who were assessed as proficient compared to those assessed as needing developmental education, John Hetts asked Brongniart about the potential inequity of how students are assessed for placement into CUNY ASAP and the related consequences for understanding the effectiveness of the program. She replied that when CUNY ASAP began in 2007, students with developmental education needs at the time of application were not accepted. However, because of the relationship CUNY ASAP now has with CUNY Start (which addresses developmental education needs in the prematriculation space), this issue of inequity in access to the program has been alleviated. She added that CUNY is moving toward broader reforms that would, for example, abandon the use of ACCUPLACER in favor of multiple measures assessments to determine student placement. In terms of the relationship among assessment, access, and program outcomes, Brongniart said that effectiveness is not studied by program component—CUNY ASAP has been and will likely continue to be studied as a comprehensive model. She commented that the ultimate goal is to transform CUNY ASAP from a "program model" to standard practice infused throughout all the areas of operation on each campus.

6

Vision for the Future and Possible Next Steps

Throughout the 2-day workshop, participants engaged in a series of discussions about possible avenues for continued research (see Box 6-1) in the ongoing journey to reform developmental mathematics education and increase success for all students. On the second day of the workshop, participants divided into four groups (two planning committee members acted as facilitators for each group) to discuss the future of developmental mathematics education. Each group was asked to depict its visions for mathematics education by 2030, to identify the evidence that is needed to advance these visions and track progress, and to describe the actions that could transform these visions into reality. One facilitator (i.e., planning committee member) from each group served as the group's reporter on the final panel of the workshop, which was moderated by planning committee chair Howard Gobstein. During the panel presentation, key takeaways from the four group conversations were shared. The workshop concluded with final reflections on the current state of developmental mathematics education and potential next steps to achieve a vision of reform that would best serve all students.

VISION

Group 2 facilitator and reporter Julie Phelps described a vision for developmental mathematics education by 2030, constructed by several workshop participants during the small group discussions:

> **BOX 6-1**
> **Possible Areas for Future Research Suggested by Workshop Participants[a]**
>
> - Developmental mathematics enrollment rates in current models and over time (Hodara)
> - Characteristics of developmental mathematics student populations in new models (Gobstein, Hodara, and Treisman)
> - Developmental mathematics student outcomes in the 4-year sector (Braddy, Hodara, and Melguizo)
> - Impacts of developmental mathematics reforms disaggregated by race/ethnicity and ability (Denley, Hodara, and Melguizo)
> - Range of academic needs of developmental mathematics students (Boatman and Denley)
> - Selection procedures that create inequality of opportunity for students (Schudde and Treisman)
> - High-quality classroom-level instruction (Bickerstaff, Mesa, and Strom)
> - Racism, sexism, and ableism in mathematics education (Adiredja)
> - Qualitative evidence in support of developmental mathematics education reform (Hetts, Hodara, Melguizo, and Strom)
> - Student experiences in developmental mathematics (Bickerstaff, Burdman, Phelps, and Roberts)
> - Developmental mathematics reform efforts and outcomes in the 2-year setting as compared to the 4-year setting (Braddy and Schweingruber)
> - Faculty capacity to meet developmental mathematics student needs (Bickerstaff, Braddy, Getz, Klipple, Mesa, Phelps, and Strom)
> - Limitations to reform in the higher education system (Bickerstaff and Rajan)
> - Equity and student outcomes (Adiredja, Braddy, Burdman, Dorsey, Mesa, Roberts, Strom, and Treisman)
> - Instructional reform that leads to increased student interest in mathematics (Roberts and Zachry Rutschow)
> - Articulation across K–12, 2-year, and 4-year educational systems (Gobstein, Melguizo, Schweingruber, and Treisman)
>
> [a]This list is not exhaustive; it contains a selection of research areas that emerged during the conversations at the workshop.

- All students would have equitable opportunities to learn the mathematics they need to navigate the world and achieve their life goals;
- Students would experience the power and beauty of mathematics and experience joy in doing mathematics; and
- Mathematics education would enable people to use mathematics tools effectively and ethically in integrated ways.

Group 1 facilitator and reporter Linda Braddy added to these ideas shared by Phelps, emphasizing the equity dimensions of the vision. She explained that "developmental mathematics education" would be eliminated and could be replaced by "college mathematics for all" or "mathematics literacy for all" by 2030. Demographics would no longer be barriers, a national free college model would be available, and a greater diversity of graduates would be working in high-demand fields, she continued. Barriers among K–12, 2-year, and 4-year institutions would be eliminated, with pathways aligned to span the entire spectrum of education. Braddy also emphasized that normative practice in 2030 would include new student success measures, a commitment to support and serve students effectively, and guidance (instead of placement) into appropriate rigorous pathways with academic support tailored to individual learners.

Group 4 facilitator Vilma Mesa shared more ideas on the vision for the future of mathematics education that came up during her small group's discussions:

- All faculty would be full-time status and able to provide high-quality instruction that addresses past inequalities and supports students not currently being well served.
- Professional development would be sustained, discipline- and context-specific, and inclusive of history about the discrimination of communities of people.
- Academic institutions would have a process for institutional cost/benefit analysis and would be funded and directed to support student services, advisement, faculty development, curriculum redesign, data collection and analysis, and human resources.

Building on Mesa's shared ideas, Braddy highlighted a difference in teaching loads for faculty in 2- and 4-year institutions and noted that, without additional funding, community college faculty will not have the time or the incentive to commit to achieving this vision.

Group 4 member Aditya Adiredja remarked that the mathematics education community should be critical and reflective of its language choices; for example, "college mathematics for all" does not promote the improved success of black students (see Larnell, 2016). Instead, specific attention is needed for particular groups of students, he continued. Group 2 member Cammie Newmyer explained that while she "appreciates the spirit of the phrase 'college mathematics for all,'" it can be "offensive and anxiety inducing," especially for low-income students and students of color. Phelps noted that, likewise, "developmental mathematics" often evokes emotions of failure, difference, and inferiority among students. Thus, many workshop participants suggested the development of a new, carefully chosen title for the field that would be approachable for and inclusive of all students.

Adiredja encouraged participants to consider who would be responsible for continuing to do this work and continuing this discussion in 2030.

Phelps noted that the American Mathematical Association of Two-Year Colleges' IMPACT: *Improving Mathematical Prowess and College Teaching* (2018) discusses how to create a ripple effect for these conversations. Group 1 member Heidi Schweingruber said that the National Academies are committed to taking this work forward and raising its visibility.

RESEARCH AND DATA NEEDS

Group 3 facilitator and reporter Tatiana Melguizo highlighted the additional evidence that would be needed to realize many of these proposed visions, based on what was shared by a number of participants during the small group discussions. She noted that a national dataset of student-level educational pathways is needed, and that this dataset would include K–12 through labor market data that are disaggregated by race/ethnicity and income and focus on additional educational and psychosocial (e.g., sense of belonging) outcomes. She said that data are needed to identify the students who cannot access or are not being well served by the pathways, and qualitative data, in particular, are needed to understand student race-based experiences in mathematics reform and instructional practices. Additionally, Melguizo explained that research design by 2030 would need to be broadened to include the following:

- more qualitative work to understand the context of interventions (i.e., where they are occurring), which is critical as differences in the fidelity of implementation of the interventions are observed;
- mixed methods to understand how practitioners make sense of reform and implement changes while they see on-time data related to changes in outcomes; and
- researcher–practitioner partnerships that promote collaboration among faculty, researchers, and practitioners across systems.

POSSIBLE ACTIONS FORWARD

Summarizing the ideas presented during the small group discussions, group 4 facilitator and reporter Tristan Denley shared the possible actions needed within the next 5 years to maintain momentum to achieve these visions for 2030. He highlighted the following possible action items:

- Fund and create a coordinated research agenda to codify the latest successful practices on a solid research base and to seek answers to open questions about students not yet being successful and differential effects across student groups.
- Amplify and understand students' voices and experiences.

- Develop a broad community of practice centered on continuous educational improvement.
- Cultivate faculty development initiatives at scale to address issues of equity and evidence-based instructional practice.
- Establish a coordinated national communication strategy that leverages research and champions (i.e., researchers, faculty, chairs, deans, institutional leaders, system leaders, and professional organizations) to amplify the success (through data) of current work.
- Engage accreditors as levers for change at scale.
- Revise tenure and promotion guidelines to honor reform work.
- Commence a companion discussion with other disciplines, such as English, in an effort to transform the "academic literacy for all" space.

Group 3 member April Strom proposed that members of the Mathematical Association of America's Research in Undergraduate Mathematics Education community could be leveraged to create a research agenda around mathematics education in community colleges, and Denley hoped that such a research agenda would also focus on the 4-year space. Schweingruber suggested understanding the differences of student outcomes in 2- and 4-year institutions as an important opportunity for the future.

FINAL REFLECTIONS

As the workshop drew to a close, planning committee members shared their final reflections on developmental mathematics education reform. Phelps reiterated the value of engaging faculty in discussions about the meanings of different types of student data and the associated implications for teaching during professional development. She suggested that if faculty take "ownership" of the data, they might be more likely to make changes within their classrooms. Denley described the Chancellor's Learning Scholars Program in Georgia, in which a select group of 110 faculty are paired with the University System of Georgia's Centers for Teaching and Learning (and other professional development entities). Each scholar then leads a "faculty learning community" with an additional 10–12 faculty, which includes weekly meetings to discuss "what it means to be a faculty member in a new paradigm of student success and what it means to address students' needs in a variety of ways." Championing the efforts described by Phelps and Denley to better serve students, Braddy asserted that administrators and educators are guilty of "educational malpractice" if they do not stop offering outdated, ineffective systems of mathematics instruction.

Philip Uri Treisman noted that institutional leadership is essential if institutional practices are to change—for example, administration, financial aid, student services, and tutoring centers will all need to evolve and connect. He proposed national policies to ensure that all people can participate in education, as well as local governance structures that would institute shared responsibility for the community of students jointly served by different educational sectors (e.g., K–12, 2-year institutions, and 4-year institutions). Melguizo noted that an integrated data system would enable such connections between high school and community college districts as well as between community college districts and 4-year institutions.

Planning committee chair Gobstein concluded the event by thanking participants, reflecting on the key themes of the 2-day workshop, and sharing his thoughts about next steps for mathematics education. He began his remarks by saying that mathematics is critical, and that changes in mathematics cannot and do not occur alone; they occur in structural, organizational, and systemic ways. The most powerful change agents are champions (e.g., faculty members and state leaders), he continued, whose initiatives need to be supported and whose communication should be leveraged with national platforms in engaging ways. Gobstein explained that educational leaders should be incentivized to transform, and that local adaptation is needed in order to transition from program alignment, to collaboration, and, ultimately, to the "development of more extensive and robust educational ecosystems—edusystems." He emphasized the need to "stretch ourselves—we need to think bigger, and we need to think differently." To do this will require changes in policy, organization, and practice at every level of our institutions and across our institutions and sectors, and such a change requires partnerships (e.g., Jobs for the Future, Transforming Postsecondary Education in Mathematics, Association of Public & Land-grant Universities, Achieving the Dream, and institutions of higher education), he continued, that build platforms for collaborating, learning, sharing, and tracking progress. Gobstein stressed that transformation at scale, in the form of a "larger and interactive edusystem," is one of this era's most challenging phases of education and social policy. He concluded by explaining that making progress will require collective efforts to align, connect, and "push in the same direction."

References

Aguirre, J.M., Mayfield-Ingram, K., and Martin, D.B. (2013). *The impact of identity in K-8 mathematics: Rethinking equity-based practices.* Reston, VA: National Council of Teachers of Mathematics.

American Mathematical Association of Two-Year Colleges. (2018). *IMPACT: Improving mathematical prowess and college teaching.* Available: https://c.ymcdn.com/sites/amatyc.site-ym.com/resource/resmgr/impact/AMATYC_IMPACT.pdf.

Boatman, A. (2019, March). *Differential impacts of developmental math by level of academic need.* Presented at the Workshop on Increasing Student Success in Developmental Mathematics, Washington, DC.

Boatman, A., and Long, B.T. (2018). Does remediation work for all students?: How the effects of postsecondary remedial and developmental courses vary by level of academic preparation. *Educational Evaluation and Policy Analysis, 40*(1), 29-58.

Brongniart, C. (2019, March). *CUNY ASAP: Comprehensive program components.* Presented at the Workshop on Increasing Student Success in Developmental Mathematics, Washington, DC.

Burdman, P. (2018). *The mathematics of opportunity: Rethinking the role of mathematics in educational equity.* Available: https://justequations.org/wp-content/uploads/je-report-r12-web.pdf.

Charles A. Dana Center. (2018). *A call to action—mathematics pathways: Scaling and sustaining.* Available: https://dcmathpathways.org/sites/default/files/resources/2018-09/Mathematics%20Pathways_Scaling%20and%20Sustaining_WEDNESDAY%20August%2029%5B4%5D.pdf.

Charles A. Dana Center. (2019). *What is rigor in mathematics really?* Available: https://www.utdanacenter.org/sites/default/files/2019-02/what-is-rigor-in-mathematics.pdf.

Chen, X. (2016). *Remedial coursetaking at U.S. public 2- and 4-year institutions: Scope, experiences, and outcomes* (NCES 2016-405). Available: https://nces.ed.gov/pubs2016/2016405.pdf.

Denley, T. (2019, March). *Co-requisite mathematics.* Presented at the Workshop on Increasing Student Success in Developmental Mathematics, Washington, DC.

Fields, R., and Parsad, B. (2012). *Test and cut scores used for student placement in postsecondary education: Fall 2011*. Available: https://www.nagb.gov/content/nagb/assets/documents/commission/researchandresources/test-and cut-scores-used-for-student-placement-in-postsecondary-education-fall-2011.pdf.

Fong, K.E., Melguizo, T., and Prater, G. (2015). Increasing success rates in developmental math: The complementary role of individual and institutional characteristics. *Research in Higher Education, 56*(7), 719-749.

Getz, A. (2019, March). *Dana Center Mathematics Pathways: Prepare, enable, empower*. Presented at the Workshop on Increasing Student Success in Developmental Mathematics, Washington, DC.

Gutierrez, R. (2007). (Re)defining equity: The importance of a critical perspective. In *Diversity, equity, and access to mathematical ideas*. New York: Teachers College Press.

Hatano, G., and Inagaki, K. (1986). Two courses of expertise. In H.W. Stevenson, H. Azuma, and K. Hakuta (Eds.), *A series of books in psychology. Child development and education in Japan* (pp. 262-272). New York: W.H. Freeman/Times Books/Henry Holt & Co.

Hetts, J. (2019, March). *Let Icarus fly: Multiple measures in assessment, the re-imagination of student capacity, and the road to college level for all*. Presented at the Workshop on Increasing Student Success in Developmental Mathematics, Washington, DC.

Hodara, M. (2019, March). *Understanding the developmental mathematics population: Findings from a nationally representative sample of first-time college entrants*. Presented at the Workshop on Increasing Student Success in Developmental Mathematics, Washington, DC.

Hu, S., Park, T., Mokher, C., Spencer, H., Hu, X., and Bertrand Jones, T. (2019). *Increasing momentum for student success: Developmental education redesign and student progress in Florida*. Available: http://purl.flvc.org/fsu/fd/FSU_libsubv1_scholarship_submission_1550948148_bd6a2f97.

Jenkins Webber, A. (2018). *Starting to succeed: The impact of CUNY Start on academic momentum—gateway course completion*. Available: https://www2.cuny.edu/wp-content/uploads/sites/4/media-assets/gateway_brief_final.pdf.

Kim, J. (2019, March). *CUNY Start: Maximizing the pre-matriculation space to address remedial needs*. Presented at the Workshop on Increasing Student Success in Developmental Mathematics, Washington, DC.

Klipple, K. (2019, March). *Carnegie Math Pathways, WestEd*. Presented at the Workshop on Increasing Student Success in Developmental Mathematics, Washington, DC.

Larnell, G. (2016). More than just skill: Examining mathematics identities, racialized narratives, and remediation among black undergraduates. *Journal for Research in Mathematics Education, 47*(3), 233-269.

Liston, C., and Getz, A. (2019). *The case for mathematics pathways*. Available: http://dcmathpathways.org/sites/default/files/resources/2019-03/CaseforMathPathways_20190313.pdf.

Mathematical Association of America. (2018). *MAA instructional practices guide*. Available: https://www.maa.org/sites/default/files/InstructPracGuideweb.pdf.

MMAP Team. (2018). *AB705 success rates estimates technical paper: Estimating success rates for students placed directly into transfer-level English and math courses*. Available: https://rpgroup.org/Portals/0/Documents/Projects/MultipleMeasures/Publications/MMAP_AB705_TechnicalPaper_FINAL_091518.pdf.

National Council of Teachers of Mathematics. (2019). Catalyzing change for elementary school. *Teaching Children Mathematics, 25*(5), 282-288.

National Research Council. (2013). *The Mathematical Sciences in 2025*. Washington, DC: The National Academies Press.

Schudde, L. (2019, March). *Who gets access to reformed dev-ed math? Evidence from Dana Center Mathematics Pathways*. Presented at the Workshop on Increasing Student Success in Developmental Mathematics, Washington, DC.

Schudde, L., and Keisler, K. (2019). The relationship between accelerated dev-ed coursework and early college milestones: Examining college momentum in a reformed mathematics pathway. *American Educational Research Association Open, 5*(1), 1-22. https://journals.sagepub.com/doi/pdf/10.1177/2332858419829435.

Scrivener, S., Gupta, H., Weiss, M. J., Cohen, B., Cormier, M. S., and Brathwaite, J. (2018). *Becoming college ready*. https://www.mdrc.org/sites/default/files/CUNY_START_Interim_Report_FINAL_0.pdf.

Strom, A. (2019, March). *Focusing on high quality instruction*. Presented at the Workshop on Increasing Student Success in Developmental Mathematics, Washington, DC.

U.S. Department of Education. (2017). *Developmental education: Challenges and strategies for reform*. Washington, DC: Office of Planning Evaluation and Policy Development.

Xu, D., and Dadgar, M. (2018). How effective are community college remedial math courses for students with the lowest math skills? *Community College Review, 46*(1), 62-81.

Xu, D., and Jaggars, S. S. (2014). Performance gaps between online and face-to-face courses: Differences across types of students and academic subject areas. *The Journal of Higher Education, 85*(5), 633-659.

Zachry Rutschow, E. (2019, March). *Developmental mathematics reforms*. Paper commissioned for the Workshop on Increasing Student Success in Developmental Mathematics, Washington, DC.

Zachry Rutschow, E. and Mayer, A. (2018). *Early findings from a national survey on developmental education practices*. New York: CAPR.

Appendix A

Workshop Agenda

Increasing Success in Developmental Mathematics: A Workshop
Lecture Room, NAS Building
2101 Constitution Avenue, NW
Washington, DC 20418

DAY 1: MONDAY, MARCH 18

8:15 am *Check-in, Breakfast and Coffee Available*

9:00 am **Welcome and Introductions**
Heidi Schweingruber, Director, Board on Science Education
Howard Gobstein, Chair, Executive Vice President of Research, Innovation and STEM Policy at the Association of Public & Land-grant Universities (APLU)

9:15 am **Panel Discussion: The Importance of Mathematics Education**
Moderator: *Linda Braddy*, Vice President for Academic Affairs, Tarrant County College and Past Deputy Executive Director, Mathematical Association of America (MAA)

Panelists:
Mark Green, Professor, University of California, Los Angeles, and Chair, Board on Mathematical Sciences and Analytics
Nicole Smith, Research Professor and Chief Economist, Georgetown University Center on Education and the Workforce[1]
Paula Wilhite, Professor, Northeast Texas Community College and Chair of Developmental Mathematics Committee, American Mathematical Association of Two-Year Colleges (AMATYC)

9:50 am   **Questions from the Audience**

10:00 am   **The Current Landscape of Strategies to Improve Developmental Mathematics Education**
Note: Full commissioned paper for this presentation is available on the project webpage.
Elizabeth Zachry Rutschow, Senior Research Associate, MDRC

10:30 am   **Questions from the Audience**
Moderator: *Tatiana Melguizo*, Associate Professor, University of Southern California

10:45 am   **Interactive Break**
Using Post-It notes provided, (1) identify other models and approaches that have not been highlighted or (2) describe an approach that you think the field should try in order to increase student success in developmental or introductory mathematics.

11:00 am   **Educational Equity and Mathematics Reform**
Moderator: *James Dorsey*, President and CEO, College Success Foundation
Panelists:
Aditya Adiredja, Assistant Professor, University of Arizona
Pamela Burdman, Senior Project Director, The Opportunity Institute

---

[1] Unable to attend.

APPENDIX A 95

     Maxine Roberts, Assistant Director of Knowledge
      Management for Strong Start to Finish, Education
      Commission of the States
     Joanna Sanchez, Program Manager, Excelencia in
      Education

11:45 am Questions and Commentary from the Audience

12:00 pm **Lunch**

1:15 pm **Student Demographics and Course-taking Experiences in Developmental Mathematics**
     Note: Full commissioned paper for this presentation is available on the project webpage.
     Michelle Hodara, Manager of Research and Evaluation, Education Northwest

1:45 pm **Questions from the Audience**
     Moderator: *Tatiana Melguizo*, University of Southern California

2:00 pm **Digging into Data About Students' Experiences: Deepening Understandings of What Works for Whom**
     Note: Short papers are available on the project webpage as background to each presentation.
     Moderator: *Susan Bickerstaff*, Senior Research Associate, Community College Research Center at Teachers College, Columbia University
     Panelists:
     Angela Boatman, Assistant Professor, Vanderbilt University
     Toby Park-Gaghan, Associate Professor, Florida State University

2:35 pm **Questions from the Audience**

2:45 pm **Panelists:**
     John Hetts, Senior Director of Data Science, Education Results Partnership
     Lauren Schudde, Assistant Professor, The University of Texas at Austin

3:15 pm **Questions from the Audience**

3:35 pm	**Break**
3:50 pm	**Open Discussion and Reflections** Facilitator: *Julie Phelps*, Professor, Valencia College, East Campus
4:15 pm	**Reflections from the Sponsor** *Amy Kerwin*, Vice President of Educational Philanthropy, Ascendium Education Group
4:25 pm	**Day 1 Wrap Up and Looking Ahead to Day 2**
4:30 pm	**Adjourn to Networking Hour** *(light refreshments available)*

DAY 2: TUESDAY, MARCH 19

8:30 am	*Breakfast and Coffee Available*
9:00 am	**Welcome to Day 2** *Howard Gobstein*, APLU
9:10 am	**Summary of Day 1 Interactive Break** Discussant: *Susan Bickerstaff*, Community College Research Center at Teachers College, Columbia University
9:20 am	**Promising Models for Change** *Note: Short papers are available on the project webpage as background to each presentation.* Moderator: *Tristan Denley*, Executive Vice Chancellor for Academic Affairs and Chief Academic Officer, University System of Georgia Panelists: *Amy Getz*, Manager, Systems Implementation for Higher Education, Charles A. Dana Center *Jeanette Kim*, Interim University Assistant Dean, Prematriculation Programs and Program Assessment, City University of New York *Karon Klipple*, Executive Director, Carnegie Mathematics Pathways, WestEd
10:15 am	**Questions and Commentary from the Audience**
10:35 am	**Coffee Break**

APPENDIX A 97

10:50 am	**Synergy of Math Reform Efforts and Overall Strategies to Transform Undergraduate Education** Moderator: *Philip Uri Treisman*, Professor, Charles A. Dana Center, The University of Texas at Austin Panelists: *Nyema Mitchell*, Senior Program Manager, Jobs for the Future *Rahim Rajan*, Deputy Director, Bill & Melinda Gates Foundation
11:30 am	**Questions and Commentary from the Audience**
11:50 am	**Instructions for Small Group Work**
12:00 pm	**Lunch**
12:30 pm	**Move into Small Groups over Lunch**
1:30 pm	**Building Capacity to Meet the Needs of Students** Moderator: *Vilma Mesa*, Professor, University of Michigan Panelists: *Christine Brongniart*, Interim ASAP University Executive Director, City University of New York *April Strom*, Professor, Chandler–Gilbert Community College and AMATYC *Karon Klipple*, Carnegie Mathematics Pathways, WestEd
2:10 pm	**Questions and Commentary from the Audience**
2:30 pm	**Break**
2:45 pm	**Panel Discussion: Vision for the Future** Moderator: *Howard Gobstein*, APLU Panelists: *Linda Braddy*, Tarrant County College *Tristan Denley*, University System of Georgia *Tatiana Melguizo*, University of Southern California *Philip Uri Treisman*, The University of Texas at Austin[2]
3:20 pm	**Questions from the Audience**

---

[2] Julie Phelps, Valencia College, replaced Treisman as a panelist for this discussion during the workshop.

3:35 pm	**Open Final Reflections from the Audience** Facilitator: *Howard Gobstein*, APLU
3:50 pm	**Reflections from the Committee Chair**
4:00 pm	**Adjourn**

Appendix B

Biographical Sketches of Workshop Planning Committee Members and Presenters

HOWARD GOBSTEIN (*Planning Committee Chair*) is the executive vice president of the Association of Public & Land-grant Universities, where he is responsible for research policy and STEM education—with their affiliated groups and portfolio of funded projects. His past positions include associate vice president for governmental affairs and director of federal relations at Michigan State University, senior policy analyst in the Office of Science and Technology in the Executive Office of the President, vice president and senior program officer at the Association of American Universities and director of federal relations for research at the University of Michigan. He has also designed and led evaluations of government science programs and policies with the U.S. Government Accountability Office. He is a fellow of the American Association for the Advancement of Science. He earned a B.S. in interdisciplinary engineering at Purdue University and an M.A. in science, technology, and public policy at The George Washington University.

ADITYA ADIREDJA (*Presenter*) is an assistant professor of mathematics education in the Mathematics Department at the University of Arizona. His research interests lie at the intersection of mathematical cognition, equity, and undergraduate mathematics, and his work focuses on understanding ways that deficit social narratives along with our perspectives on knowledge and learning impact the way that we look at mathematical sense making by students of color. He holds a B.S. and an M.S. in mathematics and a Ph.D. in mathematics education from the University of California, Berkeley.

SUSAN BICKERSTAFF (*Planning Committee Member*) is a senior research associate with the Community College Research Center. She conducts qualitative research on developmental education reform, teaching and learning, faculty learning and engagement, and student experiences at community colleges. Her dissertation focused on the experiences of adolescents at an urban community college. She has previously worked as a coordinator at a community-based adult education program and served as a research assistant on studies in family literacy. She holds a B.A. in community health from Brown University, an M.S. in education from Drexel University, and a Ph.D. in reading, writing, and literacy from the University of Pennsylvania.

ANGELA BOATMAN (*Presenter*) is an assistant professor of public policy and higher education at Vanderbilt University. Her research explores the outcomes of policies designed to increase college completion for populations traditionally underrepresented in higher education. She is currently conducting several studies on the impact of innovations in the delivery of remedial courses. She is a faculty affiliate of the Center for the Analysis of Postsecondary Readiness, housed at the Community College Research Center at Teachers College, and an affiliate of the Center for Education Policy Research at Harvard University. Boatman holds an Ed.D. with a concentration in higher education from Harvard University.

LINDA BRADDY (*Planning Committee Member*) is vice president for academic affairs at Tarrant County College (TCC) Northeast Campus. She previously served as deputy executive director of the Mathematical Association of America in Washington, DC. She was formerly dean of the Division of Health and Natural Sciences at TCC's South Campus and before that, dean of the Division of Mathematics and Natural Sciences on South Campus. Braddy has also been a professor and chair of the Department of Mathematics at East Central University in Ada, Oklahoma, where she directed professional development programs for K–12 mathematics teachers and other grant-funded initiatives to improve the teaching and learning of mathematics. She received her Ph.D. in mathematics from the University of Oklahoma, with a research focus in undergraduate mathematics education.

CHRISTINE BRONGNIART (*Presenter*) is the interim university executive director of the City University of New York's Accelerated Study in Associate Programs. She was formerly the national director of funded initiatives at the Girl Scouts of the USA, where she developed and scaled leadership development programs for girls impacted by the criminal justice system. She holds a B.A. in psychology from the University of Notre Dame and an M.S. in nonprofit management from the New School University.

PAMELA BURDMAN *(Presenter)* is the senior project director for The Opportunity Institute and founder of the Just Equations project. Working at the intersection of education research, policy, and practice, Burdman synthesizes knowledge from the field to define problems and advance strategies that support student success. Burdman has authored several reports and numerous articles on the role of mathematics as a gateway to educational opportunity, including the three-part *Degrees of Freedom* series. As a program officer for the William and Flora Hewlett Foundation, she created and implemented the foundation's investment strategies for strengthening college readiness and community college student success in California, helping to generate several statewide initiatives that continue today.

TRISTAN DENLEY *(Planning Committee Member)* currently serves as executive vice chancellor for academic affairs and chief academic officer at the University System of Georgia. His recent work focuses on transforming developmental education and advising at a system scale, and uses a data-informed approach to implement a wide variety of system scale initiatives surrounding college completion. Previous positions include vice chancellor for academic affairs at the Tennessee Board of Regents, vice president for academic affairs at Austin Peay State University, and chair of Mathematics and senior fellow of the Residential College program at the University of Mississippi. He is the creator of Degree Compass, a course recommendation system that pairs current students with the courses that best fit their talents and program of study for upcoming semesters. In 2007, he was chosen as a Redesign Scholar by the National Center for Academic Transformation for his work in rethinking the teaching of freshman mathematics classes. Denley earned his Ph.D. in mathematics from Trinity College, University of Cambridge.

JAMES DORSEY *(Planning Committee Member)* is president and chief executive officer of College Success Foundation (CSF), where his work focuses on improving educational equity for underserved students. This includes leadership of national, statewide, and campus-based programs with a focus on promoting historically underrepresented communities into science, technology, engineering, and mathematics fields, as well as the expansion of CSF's college services program, which leverages a unique combination of individualized advising and broad-based online and digital resources to support CSF scholars to college completion. Previously, he was executive director of Washington Mathematics, Engineering, Science Achievement (MESA) and president of MESA USA where his leadership and work involved cultivating strategic partnerships with the aim of improving educational outcomes for diverse student populations. Dorsey has a B.S. in geology and an M.A from California State University, Chico.

AMY GETZ (*Presenter*) is the manager for systems implementation for higher education at The University of Texas at Austin, where she leads a team that develops tools and services to support local leaders and works with external organizations to coordinate and mobilize efforts to support math pathways. Her work focuses on supporting systems and institutions to modernize entry-level college mathematics programs, and ranges from addressing obstacles in state policy to changing institutional practices and improving mathematics curriculum and instruction. She led the development of the Quantway™ curriculum in partnership with the Carnegie Foundation for the Advancement of Teaching. As the founding director of the Freshman Mathematics Program at Fort Lewis College in Durango, Colorado, she taught developmental and freshman-level math and led curriculum redesign that resulted in significant improvements in student success in both developmental and college-level math courses. Getz holds a B.A. in English theater from Fort Lewis College and an M.A in secondary school counseling from Adams State College.

MARK GREEN (*Presenter*) is a distinguished research professor in the Department of Mathematics at the University of California, Los Angeles. He was a founding co-director and later director of the National Science Foundation (NSF)-funded Institute for Pure and Applied Mathematics. He is a fellow of the American Academy of Arts and Sciences, the American Association for the Advancement of Science, and the American Mathematical Society. Green served as vice chair of the Board on Mathematical Sciences and Analytics study on *The Mathematical Sciences in 2025*. He serves on the Board of Governors of Transforming Postsecondary Education in Math and served on the Advisory Committee of the Association for Women in Mathematics. He is the chair of the National Academies' Board on Mathematical Sciences and Analytics and is the host for its monthly Mathematical Frontiers webinar.

JOHN HETTS (*Presenter*) is the senior director of data science at Educational Results Partnership and a member of the Multiple Measures Assessment Project (MMAP) research team, the California Guided Pathways Advisory Committee, and the statewide AB705 Implementation Workgroup in California. He is also a Complete College America fellow and a California Educational Policy fellow. Formerly, he was the director of institutional research at Long Beach City College during its implementation of multiple measures-based assessment. His work on predictive modeling of student assessment and placement won the 2012 RP Group Best College Research Award (with Andrew Fuenmayor and Karen Rothstein), the 2014 Association of California Community College Administrators Mertes Award (with Andrew Fuenmayor), and the 2015 RP Group Best

Statewide Research Award (as part of the MMAP research team). He received his Ph.D. in social psychology with a specialization in measurement and psychometrics from the University of California, Los Angeles, and holds a B.A. with distinction and honors from Stanford University.

MICHELLE HODARA (*Presenter*) is a manager of research and evaluation at Education Northwest. Hodara leads a Regional Educational Laboratory (REL) Northwest research-practice partnership that brings together Oregon education stakeholders from across sectors to focus on high school graduation and postsecondary success and is also the applied research lead for the REL, helping to support authors with conceptualizing and conducting their research studies. Hodara is trained in quantitative methods for program evaluation, and much of her research and evaluation focuses on postsecondary readiness and success and key issues affecting community colleges, including developmental education. Prior to earning her doctorate, she was a special education teacher in Zuni, New Mexico, and a developmental education instructor at the University of New Mexico–Gallup. Hodara holds a Ph.D. in economics and education from Teachers College, Columbia University.

AMY KERWIN (*Presenter*) is the vice president of education philanthropy at Ascendium Education Group. In this role, she leads the implementation of Ascendium's philanthropic strategy to elevate opportunities and outcomes for learners from low-income backgrounds so they can better achieve the postsecondary education and career goals that matter most to them. Prior to joining Ascendium in 1994, Kerwin spent 4 years as an auditor at EY. She is both a certified public accountant and a certified internal auditor. Kerwin serves on the boards of Grantmakers for Education and the Wisconsin Philanthropy Network and is a member of the Wisconsin Governor's Council on Financial Literacy. She holds a B.S. in accountancy from the University of Wisconsin–La Crosse.

JEANETTE KIM (*Presenter*) is currently the interim university assistant dean for prematriculation programs and program assessment at CUNY, overseeing three major prematriculation program areas: CUNY Start, the Adult Literacy Programs, and the CUNY Language Immersion Programs. She also oversees the Research, Evaluation, and Program Support team, which provides program evaluation services to more than 30 different programs administered by CUNY's Central Office. Previous positions include assistant dean for high school partnerships at State University of New York (SUNY) Westchester Community College and deputy director of collaborative programs at CUNY, where she was responsible for the management and oversight of CUNY's dual enrollment and pre-college STEM initiatives. Kim has a B.S. in biology and chemistry from SUNY Albany and an M.A. in educational administration and policy from Teachers College, Columbia University.

KARON KLIPPLE (*Presenter*) is executive director of the Carnegie Math Pathways program at WestEd (formerly at the Carnegie Foundation for the Advancement of Teaching.) In this role, she leads a networked improvement community of more than 100 colleges across the country working collectively to help students learn mathematics in ways that emphasize practical skills that will serve them in the future. She is part of the core team that launched this network in 2010, and under her leadership, the program's outcomes have continued to increase as it has scaled to tens of thousands of students across a variety of instructional settings. Klipple has almost 20 years of experience in teaching and mathematics program reform, most recently at San Diego City College where she was associate professor of mathematics, and 5 years of experience as a product manager for scientific software. She has taught statistics and mathematics at the community college, high school, and university level. She holds a B.A. in mathematics from Trinity University and a Ph.D. in statistics from Texas A&M University.

TATIANA MELGUIZO (*Planning Committee Member*) is an associate professor in the University of Southern California Rossier School of Education. She works in the field of economics of higher education. She uses quantitative methods of analysis and large-scale longitudinal survey data to study the association of different factors such as student trajectories and specific institutional characteristics on the persistence and educational outcomes of minority (African American and Hispanic) and low-income students. She is a recipient of the American Education Research Association dissertation grant as well as grants from the Institute of Education Sciences, Spencer Foundation, the Bill & Melinda Gates Foundation, Jack Kent Cooke, Nellie Mae, and Lumina Foundations, the Association for Institutional Research, and the National Postsecondary Education Cooperative. Melguizo received her M.A. in social policy from the London School of Economics and her Ph.D. in economics of education from Stanford University.

VILMA MESA (*Planning Committee Member*) is professor of education, faculty associate at the Center for the Study of Higher and Postsecondary Education, and professor of mathematics at the University of Michigan. She investigates the role that resources play in developing teaching expertise in undergraduate mathematics, specifically at community colleges and in inquiry-based learning classrooms. She has conducted several analyses of instruction and of textbooks and collaborated in evaluation projects on the impact of innovative mathematics teaching practices for students in

STEM. She has been principal investigator in National Science Foundation and Institute for Education Sciences funded projects, a Fulbright Scholar, and a research associate at "una empresa docente," a research center in mathematics education at the University of Los Andes, Bogotá, Colombia, where she co-authored university textbooks for pre-calculus for engineering and probability and statistics for social science majors. She holds a B.S. in computer science and a B.S. in mathematics from the University of Los Andes in Bogotá, Colombia, and an M.A and a Ph.D. in mathematics education from the University of Georgia.

NYEMA MITCHELL (*Presenter*) is a senior program manager with Jobs for the Future's (JFF's) postsecondary team, which works to improve student success by helping states and their community colleges dramatically increase the number of students who complete college and earn high-value credentials. Mitchell supports the national network of Student Success Centers. This work includes designing and developing services and supporting data collection and program evaluation, as well as targeted coaching and technical assistance. Prior to joining JFF, she was a researcher with the Center for Education Policy at SRI International. Mitchell has an M.S. in public policy from the Georgia Institute of Technology and a B.A. in education studies and public policy from Brown University.

TOBY PARK-GAGHAN (*Presenter*) is an associate professor of economics of education and education policy in the Department of Educational Leadership and Policy Studies, and associate director of the Center for Postsecondary Success of Florida State University. Park-Gaghan's primary research utilizes quasi-experimental methods and large statewide datasets to investigate student outcomes in postsecondary education and explore potential policy initiatives that could improve student success. Park-Gaghan is co-principal investigator on a multi-year project investigating developmental education reform in Florida, funded in part by the Bill & Melinda Gates Foundation and the Institute for Education Sciences. Park-Gaghan holds a Ph.D. in education policy from Vanderbilt University, and an M.Ed. in higher education management and a B.S. in mathematics from the University of Pittsburgh.

JULIE PHELPS (*Planning Committee Member*) is the Lockheed Martin chair of mathematics, professor of mathematics, and developmental mathematics coordinator at Valencia College. Her research focuses on ways to increase student engagement, learning, retention, self-efficacy, and success among mathematics students in the first 2 years of college. She has served as project director of Achieving the Dream, where she focused on identifying and closing achievement gaps across racial and ethnic groups, between college-ready and underprepared students, and between student success in mathematics and other discipline courses. Phelps has also served in the appointed role as communication liaison for American Mathematics Association for Two-Year Colleges (AMATYC) in connection to developmental mathematics pathways redesign and is now the chair of the AMATYC Mathematics Standards Committee. Phelps holds a B.S. from Florida Southern College and an M.S. and a Ph.D. in curriculum and instruction, specializing in community college from the University of Central Florida.

RAHIM RAJAN (*Presenter*) is the deputy director of the Bill & Melinda Gates Foundation. He leads and manages a diverse portfolio focused on helping faculty and students at postsecondary institutions benefit from high-quality, personalized digital learning. Grants that Rajan has helped launched or manage include Next Generation Learning Challenges, Next Generation Courseware Challenge, and the Adaptive Learning Market Acceleration Program. Prior to this, Rajan helped in the launch, growth, and management of three not-for-profit technology start-up organizations (JSTOR, ITHAKA, Aluka) that have transformed how higher education and cultural/research institutions around the world access, preserve, and distribute online scholarly research, monographs, primary sources, and literature. Rajan earned an M.Phil. from the University of Cambridge and his B.A. in philosophy from the University of Chicago.

MAXINE ROBERTS (*Presenter*) is dedicated to advancing system-changing, equity-focused initiatives for students who are traditionally marginalized in higher education. She has directed youth-based programs in New York City, worked with community college faculty in California to improve their course outcomes, and conducted research on the factors that contribute to success and progress for students of color in developmental mathematics. Currently, she serves as the assistant director of knowledge management for Strong Start to Finish at the Education Commission of the States. She was the recipient of the 2017–2018 AERA Minority Dissertation fellowship and the 2018 Rossier Dissertation Award of Merit. Roberts holds a Ph.D. in urban education policy from the University of Southern California and an M.A in reading and literacy specialization and English education from Bank Street College of Education and Teachers College, Columbia University.

JOANNA SANCHEZ (*Presenter*) is a program manager at Excelencia in Education. In this role, she manages the development of the Seal and Ladder of Engagement portfolio and works with institutions committed to better serving Latino students. A first-generation college graduate and Gates Millennium Scholar, Sanchez recently completed a postdoctoral research fellowship at Howard University funded by the National Science Foundation.

Previously she served as a Geographic Information Systems (GIS) professional in both the private and public sectors, including teaching GIS at South Texas College. She holds a Ph.D. in educational leadership and policy from The University of Texas at Austin, as well as an M.A. in GIS from the University of Denver and a B.S. in geosciences from Trinity University.

LAUREN SCHUDDE (*Presenter*) is an assistant professor of educational leadership and policy at The University of Texas at Austin. She is also a faculty research affiliate of the university's Population Research Center and Charles A. Dana Center and Teachers College's Community College Research Center. Her research examines the impact of educational policies and practices on college student outcomes, with ongoing projects focused on how community college students respond to institutional transfer policies and the influence of developmental education mathematics reform on student outcomes. Her work has been published in the *Sociology of Education*, *Journal of Human Resources*, *AERA Open*, *Review of Research in Education*, *Review of Higher Education*, *Research in Higher Education*, and *Community College Review*. Schudde received her Ph.D. in sociology from the University of Wisconsin–Madison.

APRIL STROM (*Presenter*) has taught mathematics at the community-college level for more than 20 years. She is currently a member of the U.S. National Commission on Mathematics Instruction and serves as the AMATYC Southwest Vice President. She has served as principal investigator (PI) and co-PI on various National Science Foundation–funded projects focused on both research in mathematics education and professional development of K–14 instructors. Strom also co-lead the writing of the Classroom Practices chapter of the *MAA Instructional Practices Guide* and served on the steering committee for the AMATYC IMPACT guide. She received her Ph.D. in curriculum and instruction (emphasis in mathematics education) from Arizona State University and holds an M.A. and a B.A. in mathematics from Texas Tech University.

PHILIP URI TREISMAN (*Planning Committee Member*) is a university distinguished teaching professor, professor of mathematics, and professor of public affairs at The University of Texas at Austin. He is the founder and executive director of the university's Charles A. Dana Center, and launched the Dana Center Mathematics Pathways. Treisman is a founding member of Transforming Post-Secondary Education in Mathematics and serves as the representative of the American Mathematical Society to the American Association for the Advancement of Science (Education, Section Q). He created the Urban Mathematics Leadership Network, has served as a distinguished senior fellow at the Education Commission of the States since 2013, and is currently the chairman of the Strong Start to Finish Campaign. He has served on the STEM working group of the President's Council of Advisors on Science and Technology, on the 21st-Century Commission on the Future of Community Colleges of the American Association of Community Colleges, and on the Commission on Mathematics and Science Education of the Carnegie Corporation of the New York Institute for Advanced Study. Treisman holds a Ph.D. in mathematics and education from the University of California, Berkeley.

PAULA WILHITE (*Presenter*) leads instruction in mathematics, physics, and engineering as division chair and professor of mathematics at Northeast Texas Community College where she is a charter faculty member. Wilhite's work actively supports the reform movement in developmental mathematics, with its focus on teaching mathematics to students from underserved populations and its emphasis on active learning, constructive persistence, and interdisciplinary application. She has served as the principal investigator for a National Science Foundation scholarship grant for students who are eligible for a federal Pell Grant. Wilhite was a member of the Course Design Team for the Mathways Project developed by the Charles A. Dana Center at The University of Texas at Austin. She was awarded the 2004 Texas Mathematical Teaching Excellence Award and the 2013 AMATYC Teaching Excellence Award. Since 2016, she has served as chair of the AMATYC Developmental Mathematics Committee, which provides a forum for the exchange of ideas to improve the quality of developmental mathematics programs in the first 2 years of college.

ELIZABETH ZACHRY RUTSCHOW (*Presenter*) is a senior research associate at MDRC where she leads research on developmental education, adult basic education, and GED preparation. She is the director of several projects in these areas: (1) an evaluation of the Dana Center Mathematics Pathways; (2) an examination of implementation and sustainability of paid internships in 33 colleges in the Midwest; and (3) a scan of promising adult basic education programs in California. She also serves as the lead for reports examining the revision of developmental education assessment and instruction across the United States, as part of the Center for the Analysis of Postsecondary Readiness. She has authored numerous reports, including two literature reviews analyzing the most promising reforms in developmental and adult education (*Unlocking the Gate* and *Beyond the GED*). Prior to joining MDRC, she worked as a researcher and teacher in adult literacy education and served as a doctoral fellow at the National Center for the Study of Adult Learning and Literacy at the Harvard Graduate School of Education. She holds an Ed.D. and an M.E. in education from the Harvard Graduate School of Education.

Appendix C

Workshop Participants[1]

Aditya Adiredja
Joseph Agnich
Diaa Ahmed
Janice Anderson
Susan Bickerstaff
Angela Boatman
Caroline Boules
Linda Braddy
Kerry Brenner
Christine Brongniart
Pamela Burdman
Leticia Bustillos
Linda Casola
Ted Coe
Jessica Covington
Tristan Denley
James Dorsey
Nikki Edgecombe
Rebecca Fitch

Leticia Garcilazo Green
Ruanda Garth-McCullough
Amy Getz
Howard Gobstein
Mark Green
Rebecca Hartzler
Mary Heiss
Robert Hershey
John Hetts
Michelle Hodara
Guy Johnson
Karen Keene
Amy Kerwin
Jeanette Kim
Karon Klipple
Steven Leinwand
Bernard Mair
Monette McIver
Tatiana Melguizo

---

[1] This list reflects the names of in-person participants only. The workshop also included a number of participants who attended by webcast.

Vilma Mesa
Nyema Mitchell
Cammie Newmyer
Toby Park-Gaghan
Michael Pearson
Julie Phelps
Rahim Rajan
Maxine Roberts
Joanna Sanchez

Lauren Schudde
Heidi Schweingruber
April Strom
Tiffany Taylor
Philip Uri Treisman
Paula Wilhite
Charles Zachry
Sherry Zachry
Elizabeth Zachry Rutschow